The Girl with the Self-Esteem Issues

ROSIE MERCADO

The Girl with the Self-Esteem Issues

A MEMOIR

ROSIE MERCADO

HarperOne
An Imprint of HarperCollins*Publishers*

HarperOne

IMAGE OF WOMAN DANCING: COSMIC_DESIGN | SHUTTERSTOCK

FIRST EDITION

Designed by Janet Evans-Scanlon

Library of Congress Cataloging-in-Publication Data

Names: Mercado, Rosie, 1980- author.
Title: The girl with the self-esteem issues: a memoir / Rosie Mercado.
Description: First edition. | San Francisco: HarperOne, 2020.
Identifiers: LCCN 2020010132 (print) | LCCN 2020010133 (ebook) | ISBN 9780062895226 (hardcover) | ISBN 9780062895301 (trade paperback) | ISBN 9780062895318 (ebook)
Subjects: LCSH: Mercado, Rosie, 1980-| Television personalities—United States Biography. | Hispanic American television personalities—Biography. | Models (Persons)—United States—Biography.
Classification: LCC PN2287.M6125 A3 2020 (print) | LCC PN2287.M6125 (ebook) | DDC 791.45/75092 [B]—dc23
LC record available at https://lccn.loc.gov/2020010132
LC ebook record available at https://lccn.loc.gov/2020010133

---

20 21 22 23 24 LSC 10 9 8 7 6 5 4 3 2 1

CONTENTS

INTRODUCTION

The Girl with the Self-Esteem Issues

HOLA, MAMACITA. I'M SO GLAD YOU'RE HERE.

I wrote this book you're holding in your hands right now, and I'm so excited you're reading it. There's been a lot going on around here (some of it exciting, some pretty crazy), and I've lost count of the number of times I've been told, "You should write a book." For a while it wasn't something I even wanted to think about. I consider myself a positive person, but to be honest, I was on a pretty rocky road—going through a lot of sh*t, to put it plainly. My life has changed; I am a life coach now, and as I remember some of my experiences, my deepest desire is to be a support to others who are facing their *own* challenges. If telling my story can keep anyone from being as clueless as I was, or get others to start showing up for themselves, I'm here for that.

So. There's a lot to tell. There are my three kids. And my husbands. Well, *ex*-husbands. There's my unlikely modeling career. My unexpected, amazing, true love story. That time I almost died. And . . . Wait . . .

Breathe, Rosie.

Okay. I think I'm getting ahead of myself here. Where to begin my story?

I guess I should start the way I start most things . . . with a large cup of freshly brewed dark Mexican coffee.

No one makes better authentic Mexican coffee than my mom. When you wake up in my mom's house, you are greeted by the smell of coffee and cinnamon—one of my favorite smells ever. If I close my eyes for just a minute, I can conjure up the warmth of that aroma along with an image of my mom bustling about preparing coffee for my dad. Coffee wasn't just a breakfast drink—my mom also always made it in the evening after dinner. While we kids did our homework, Mom and Dad would sit at the table in the kitchen, sip their coffee, and talk—discussing their day, their concerns, and their joys. To me, this routine of theirs was emblematic of something I deeply craved: a mature love. They loved each other, they were fierce about their family, they communicated, they had shared goals and dreams, and they were working together to manifest them. Like all couples, they didn't always agree, but watching them, I could see how they handled their disagreements with a sense of respect and space. And they would always make up before they went to bed!

The truth is that my dad was something of a drill sergeant. He has a strong character. But he's a gentleman, he always makes time for my mom, and she softens his personality. One of my favorite memories of my parents is walking behind them and seeing my dad reach for my mom's hand. Even as a little girl, I liked looking at them holding hands. My image of my dad has always been that of strength and protection. As long as my dad was there, I knew everything was all good. But there has never been any question about whether my parents, who are also business partners, are connected by something stronger than family, children, house, bills, and daily life—they have always had *love.* I could see it. And that's what I've always wanted for myself.

You might not realize it, but love is what's brought you and me together. Here. Underneath it all, it's the real reason I wrote this book. Surprised? Yes, I know, the title is *The Girl with the Self-Esteem Issues.* And believe me, we'll get to those. But more than that, this is a book about love. Love was always my ultimate goal in life—something I always wanted to give as well as receive.

Turns out, love isn't always easy. And I'm probably the last person anyone would expect to write a book that includes advice for anybody else, because I have had my share of ups and downs in that department (see the previous mention of my ex-husbands). Also, for most of my life, I've been called names because of my weight. And I let it affect how I viewed myself. When I first became a plus-size model, I weighed over four hundred pounds. (Even after losing two hundred pounds, people still call me fat.) And I'm Latina. I'm a woman. There have been many times when I've had little or no money in my bank account. I've had to walk away from certain people. I've had to *run* away from others. I know what it means to be in an abusive relationship—to be afraid of a man who is throwing things at me or putting his hands around my neck. I've spent the majority of my life being "the girl with the self-esteem issues." And yet, here I am.

But here's a secret: The best advice doesn't come from someone who got it right the first time; it comes from people who have seen some serious sh*t and learned what they know the hard way. It comes from those of us who have messed up and had to start again—those of us who know what it is to struggle with the odds working against us, but who have still been able to wake up day after day to fight, scrape, and claw our way to the life we want.

And it all comes back to love.

Yes, at some point in our lives, most of us crave a true partner like what my mom and dad have—a person with whom we can have a lifelong, devoted relationship. But there is an even more important and essential kind of love: self-love.

I know, I know. Self-love is *difficult*. For everybody, not just for women. And not only for those of us with self-esteem issues. But self-love is what transformed me, and it's my hope that when you read about my life, you'll get some inspiration that will help you transform your own life too.

Time to Do Things Differently

A well-known and all-too-true motivational quote that I heard first from Tony Robbins made a big impression on me: *If you do what you've always done, you'll get what you've always gotten.*

True, right?

How about you? Are you familiar with the feeling of doing the same thing over and over again, expecting a different result?

Maybe there's a promotion you've been chasing for years that your boss keeps dangling in front of you. Maybe you've wanted to go back to school or get better grades but always find yourself putting off registration or not making time for studying and then—surprise!—getting the same result. Maybe you want to lose weight. Find a partner. Learn a language. Write a book. Take a vacation to the Galápagos Islands. Start a business. Attract tons of abundance (money). Save the rain forest. Whatever it is you want to do, I promise you one thing: *If you do what you've always done, you'll get what you've always gotten.*

To change the story of your life, you have to change your behavior. We all have stories that we tell ourselves about who we are, right? In my case, the story I told myself was that I was a failure—a four-hundred-plus-pound abandoned mother of three who had been physically and emotionally abused, not to mention cheated on. If I wanted to change my life—*and get a different result*—I had to change my behavior . . . and thereby, my story. And I had to believe that I could do it. Yes, I had goals I dreamed about achieving, but my behavior was standing in my way. I wasn't doing enough to help myself. In fact, I was often so depressed that after I got the kids to school, I would lock myself in my room and cry. I would isolate myself. Even though I was aware that doing this was setting up a vicious cycle, I kept doing it. It was part of my daily go-to pattern of depression.

If I wanted to get where I wanted to go, I had to focus on the behaviors that needed changing: Stop emotional eating. Stop feeling so sorry for myself. I needed to start becoming more self-aware—about what I was thinking as well as what I was doing. I had to pay attention and notice whenever I felt guilt or self-blame. I needed to learn to give those feelings a moment and then ask them kindly to get the f*ck out. I had to examine my negative thinking and call myself out on my own excuses. Losing all my bullsh*t excuses was an important and essential first step. I had to start moving in the direction I wanted to go.

When I first started modeling, I often told myself that I was never going to be able to book enough modeling assignments at my weight, so why should I waste my time trying? No matter how much I dieted, I was never going to be a size 4, so why should I try to lose weight? I was never going to be able to control my shopping and my spending, so why even try to save money? I imagine you have some problems of your own, so you understand where I was coming from. We all have problems.

Life has handed me some hard-won lessons. Because of them I learned the importance of self-examination and self-awareness. Brutal self-honesty is a secret weapon we can all use to get where we want to go. It helped me beat my self-esteem issues against tremendous odds. I now work full-time helping other people go after what they want. I will do whatever I can to help others make healthier decisions. If we want to change our lives, we have to be willing to own our issues and unhealthy patterns. We have to give up all those self-limiting ideas and self-defeating behaviors. Remember: **None of us can keep doing things the same way and expect different results.**

Boy, did I learn that truth the hard way. But let me say, in all gratitude, that learning the hard way has given me something valuable to offer here: how to stand up for yourself, be your best friend, fight the good fight, and practice self-love every single day. Every chapter in this book includes a lesson I learned through pain and struggle;

you get to hear all the juicy details about how I totally screwed up before learning that lesson for myself.

Sometimes when everything appears to be at its worst—times when you're going through experiences and feelings that you wouldn't wish on anyone else—know that you are being given a wake-up call to change and improve your life. This is the time when you must ask yourself: What am I supposed to learn from this situation? How can I change and grow for the better? What can I be grateful for? You can't be both grateful and resentful. You can only live in one place. Which will you choose?

If you have any kind of a belief system, and I certainly do, you have an intrinsic understanding that all the things that happen to us are not completely accidental. Throughout life, we are supposed to learn, change, and grow. We are supposed to become better, more loving, and more empathetic human beings. When you're trudging through a really bad period in your life, it might help to start seeing these times—days, weeks, months, or even years—as providing opportunities for personal growth.

Think about some of the dramas, traumas, and bad moments in your own life. Perhaps you've experienced a breakup or divorce, health crisis, financial setback, or the loss of a loved one. These are painful experiences—but they all contain real and important lessons. When things aren't going right in your life, always remember to stop and ask yourself: What's my lesson here? What is life trying to tell me? Pay attention, and try to figure it all out. Can you use your negative experiences to help you change and transform your life for the better?

Now, before you head to chapter 1, I want to tell you one more thing. The other day I was hanging out at my parents' house with my three kids. We were clearing the table after a delicious dinner, preparing Mexican coffee, and suddenly the smell took me back to a time when I was a child heading off to play with my brother and sisters while my mom got to watch one of her favorite telenovelas, and Pops, as always, was busy fixing something around the house. Thinking of myself as a child made me realize there was one thing I wish I had known at that time.

I wish that I had known how to approach life with more of a "F*ck it, I'm just going to do it!" attitude. It took me a lot of years before I was able to go for what I wanted. I was always so caught up in what others thought about me and what they would say about me—it filled me with stupid, foolish fears, and I allowed it to limit my ability to follow my dreams. I needed to say, "F*ck it," and push myself toward my goals without worrying about what others thought or whether I was doing things right. Of course we all make mistakes. The important thing is that we are able to learn from them and self-correct.

Whatever you are going through right now, there is a reason for it. And I truly believe God will reveal that reason when the time is right. In the meantime, as long as your goals are positive and life-affirming, why not say, "F*ck it, I'm just going to do it"? Own your strength, and move on it. Even if you are scared, you can change the energy and direction of your life. This is about loving yourself and taking a chance on yourself and your future.

I did it, and you can do it too . . .

CHAPTER 1

Change Your Damn Story

MY DAD KEPT ASKING ME, "ROSIE, ARE YOU OKAY? ARE YOU okay?"

Huh? I wondered. Am I okay? What a crazy question. Of course I'm not okay. I haven't been okay in years. I haven't been okay for a decade.

It dawned on me that I was in a hospital room, waking up from some sort of medication-induced sleep. My vision was blurry. My thoughts were desperate. I could barely move my arms and legs, and my words were slurry. I didn't try to talk for fear that I would stutter or everything would come out garbled. I knew that saying something, anything, would reassure my dad and that that was what I needed to do. But I couldn't form the words.

No, I'm not okay, I thought.

My dad stared at me, searching for any sign of the fighter he knew his daughter could be. He touched my head, pushed some hair off my forehead like he had when I was a kid with a fever. But I was no longer a little girl; I was a twenty-eight-year-old woman, and I had just been told that I had a cyst on my brain.

"*Confianza en Dios,*" Dad said quietly, but with some force. *Trust God.*

My eyes—empty, lost, sad—looked back at him. It was the blank stare of a defeated woman who had totally, completely, unapologetically *given up.*

It had been a long, scary haul with this most recent issue. Out of nowhere, I'd been having balance problems. I teetered and tripped and had to grab on to anything near me to stay upright. My speech was off—it was worse when I first woke up in the morning, but even later in the day I would stutter or slur my words. It was obvious there was something very wrong with me, and my dad had taken charge.

He first took me to a hospital in Las Vegas, where I was given a prescription for Valium to treat what they thought was anxiety. Then we saw other Vegas doctors, who basically attributed any problems I was having to my weight. My blood pressure was extremely high, and I was close to having a stroke. I felt helpless, but my dad was undaunted. After some more research, he found a doctor in Mexico, and off we went again. That is my father: totally action-oriented. Whatever is happening, he is going to deal with it head on. In his view, this was no time for emotion—we had to get answers. Whatever it took, wherever he had to drive me, he was going to handle this. I was very grateful knowing that my mom was looking after my kids, so at least that worry was covered.

There isn't much I remember about that time in the hospital except that I was terrified that I was going to die. I was convinced that my supportive parents would lose their oldest daughter and my three beautiful children were going to grow up without a mother. What was going to happen to them? I couldn't help but feel angry at their fathers. They were off leading their lives, doing what they wanted. Why was I here sick? And what about my dreams?

Were they finished?

And yet, as I gazed back at my dad, feeling a nauseating dizziness from my head to my toes, feeling like I was going to die, in the back of my mind another thought was creeping in.

I have to change.

This was something that I suddenly knew in every cell of my being. If I wanted to get out of this alive, I was going to have to change my ways. Do something different. Otherwise, I. Was. Always. Going. To. Get. The. Same. Result.

I thought about my fat ass. My hips. My thighs. All the extra weight that had been hanging off my body as well as my psyche for most of my life.

My *caderas y nalgas*—that part of me that suddenly appeared when I was still in elementary school and kept me from wearing short shorts like the other girls. From fifth grade on, I was known as the girl with the fat ass, and other kids called me a variety of mean and hurtful names, most of which featured my ass.

I have always had issues with food. My behavior gave new meaning to the term "emotional eater." Even when I was a child, food became something I turned to under just about any circumstance. When I was happy, I wanted to sit down with somebody I cared about, share my joy, and have something to eat. When I was sad, I moved toward the refrigerator, hoping to drown my sorrows in something yummy. I would start the day with tortillas still warm from the oven and slathered with fresh butter. Didn't everything seem better when I was eating rice pudding? (Lots of it!) When I needed comfort, what was more satisfying than some huevos rancheros with rice and beans and a few more tortillas on the side? I loved beans—all kinds: black, red, refried; they are basically Mexican caviar to me. If I needed more spice in my life, I added some salsa roja and just chowed down. When I wanted to talk to someone, I always found it easier to communicate if I was enjoying *café de olla,* with a few *galletas* or even a beautiful piece of pan dulce.

Do I even need to mention my metabolism or my genetic inclination to gain weight? Growing up, I remember relatives who weighed close to five hundred pounds and could hardly move. I always loved my family, and I certainly understood how easy it was to gain weight. But I didn't want to be like that. Was I going to turn out that way?

By the time I was twelve, I was embarrassed and ashamed of my weight. I wanted so much to be thin like the other girls at school, but I didn't know how to achieve this objective. I couldn't have been more than thirteen when I told my mother that I needed to lose weight. She was supportive, and I went on a well-advertised diet plan—the kind where you order the food and all your meals are delivered ready to be prepared. And the pounds disappeared when I stuck to the plan, but it was almost impossible to do what was necessary to assemble and fix the meals when I was at school, and at home I was surrounded by people who were eating regular food. Bottom line, the minute I tried to transition back to eating like everybody else, I gained back all the weight I had lost, plus some.

At twenty-eight and hospitalized for a brain cyst, I was heavier than I'd ever been and understood body shaming like nobody's business. Body shaming is endemic in our society, and I get that it doesn't just happen to people who are overweight. I remember once talking to a client who told me that her mother used to chase her around the kitchen trying to get her to eat, all the while screaming, "Look at you! You're so skinny no man will ever want you." But I'm not talking about the kind of body shaming that we do to others or that they do to us. I'm talking about the most destructive form of body shaming: all the times we have unkind and harsh opinions about our own appearance.

Most of my self-esteem issues revolved around my weight, but I realize other people focus on different parts of their bodies. I've spoken to women who can't stop thinking about chins, noses, breasts, butts, or even their skin. I've also spoken to *thin* women whose self-esteem issues have helped convince them that they are *fat*.

There have been serious studies showing women's confidence in their bodies is declining; low body esteem is a condition shared by women and girls around the world. One large study of more than ten thousand females published by Dove showed that nearly all women (85 percent) and girls (79 percent) said they opt out of life activities—such as trying out for a team or club, and engaging with family or loved ones—when they don't feel good about the way they look.

Girls and women who worry about their weight don't need studies to tell them that they avoid going places and having fun because of concerns with body image. The simplest activity, from walking on a beach to going to a party with friends, can become fraught with anxieties. Where can I find something to wear? Will it fit? Will my stomach stick out? How about my thighs? Breasts? Butt? Tell me the truth—is my ass jiggling? Do my arms look funny? When I stand next to my very thin friend, will I feel embarrassed? Will she?

If you are struggling with self-esteem, the question of what to wear and how to be comfortable at social events can be a continuing and stressful headache. However, this difficulty pales in comparison to the other problems one might face. As I discovered, it's all too easy for girls and women to make questionable or even downright bad life choices and decisions because of the lowered self-esteem that accompanies troubled body image issues. I figured out, and many other women would agree, that it sometimes seems as though low self-esteem actually attracts destructive romantic partners and friends who prey on vulnerability.

So how could I not think about my ass? No one would let me forget about it.

When I first arrived at the hospital, dizzy with a pounding chest and almost no sense of balance, I didn't know what was wrong. Neither did the doctors, who immediately started running tests.

When all the heart and blood tests came back normal, the doctors decided that I needed an MRI so they could better assess my condition. Almost as soon as I arrived at the radiology department, however, it was apparent something was delaying the procedure. Two of the technicians were standing there looking perplexed. I could tell that they were trying to figure out how to get me from the wheelchair to the machine. And there was yet another problem. The technicians looked at me; they looked at the MRI; they had a brief whispered conference. Nobody actually pulled out a tape measure, but that's how it felt. Finally the technicians left the room and came back with a young-looking resident. He was the one who made the final pronouncement.

"She won't fit."

I want to pause right here. This was not the first time that I'd been told I wouldn't "fit." And it wouldn't be the last. I had a difficult time fitting into some cars, as well as seats in movie theaters. I absolutely could not fit in amusement park rides. If any of my children ever wanted to go on a Ferris wheel or roller coaster, I knew I wouldn't be able to go with them. When I agreed to meet somebody in a restaurant, I would drive there to scope it out in the days beforehand to make sure that it didn't have tight booths. But my problems with "fit" weren't limited to physical space. When I first went to school, there were very few other Latinos, and some of my classmates made it very clear that they didn't think I fit in. When I was modeling, I didn't fit the mold of a plus-size 14, not to mention a straight model size 4. Not "fitting" has been a recurring part of my life. During my marriages, there were times when I was mentally, emotionally, and physically abused, and I didn't want to tell anyone because I was ashamed. I didn't speak up, I stayed home, I cooked, I cleaned, I lost my voice, I lost my power. I put up with disrespect; I obviously didn't fit the image my ex-husbands had for a wife. At school events, I was often the only single mom in a room full of married couples. "Fitting" has never been something I've done very well.

At least the problem of not fitting into the MRI could be resolved by sending me to a facility with a larger machine, which is what happened. That's when I finally received a diagnosis. I was told that a fluid-filled sac had formed on the right side of my brain. This cyst had been causing my recent problems with coordination—the stuttering and slurring and having to grab hold of things to steady myself.

The recommended treatment for a brain cyst is surgical removal. I wasn't thrilled at the idea of somebody operating on or near my brain, and the doctors told me straightaway that my weight made the surgery even riskier. But instead of thinking about the risks of surgery, I was thinking how embarrassing it was that I was probably too fat to have an operation of any kind.

My own self-esteem had hit rock bottom. I was a master of self-hatred. I was emotionally distraught; I was spiritually disconnected. I didn't even like my own thoughts. I played movies out in my mind about things that hadn't even happened. I was lonely. Who was I? What would I become?

And so there I was in the lowest moment of my life, with my dad looking into my eyes. "Rosie, what are you thinking?" he asked.

I asked myself the same question: Rosie, what are you thinking? I wanted to scream, to cry. I prayed for God to take this dizziness and fear away. I was praying like crazy:

"Dios mío, ayúdame."

I could not let this be the end of my life. There was so much I had wanted to do and see. I had dreams. I wanted to be a professional model; I wanted to be on television; but first I needed to work on myself.

At the edge of death and despair, I could see everything with greater clarity. What did I need to do to help myself? Thinking about the mistakes I had already made, I realized every major decision I'd made in my life to date had been the result of self-esteem issues. I resolved in that moment that if I were to make it off that hospital bed and find a way to live, I would change. I would choose to fiercely love myself. I would stop letting low self-esteem get in the way of my dreams and I would finally have the life I'd always wanted.

And then, as if my desperate thoughts had made their way to my home in Las Vegas, my phone rang. It was my daughter, Bella. When her sweet voice asked how I felt, I could hear her genuine worry and concern. In the background, I could hear hustle and bustle going on around her. I could imagine my precious Valentino, born with cerebral palsy as well as an indomitable spirit. He was extremely challenged in his daily activities. At that point in his life, he couldn't even lift his head and was dependent on me for everything. I watched his every move, always worried about his ability to breathe and stay alive. If I wasn't there, one of my parents was always with him. What would happen to Valentino if something happened to me? And how about my youngest child—bright, funny, and hyperactive Alex, who was just learning to walk and couldn't sit still?

After Bella hung up, I felt as if I had just received a hug from heaven. My children were my proof that something good could come out of anything—even disastrously failed relationships. I thought about my parents and looked over at my dad. I experienced a sudden rush of gratitude. I was living in my parents' house and trying to support my children as a makeup artist while also working a full-time job in my father's office. I knew I was overly dependent on my parents, whom I had disappointed more times than I cared to remember.

Change. Change. Change. It was as necessary as air.

Did I need to fit in, be like everyone else? No, I didn't even want that.

I looked down at my body—at the hips that wouldn't fit in an MRI machine but had given birth to three babies and carried this woman (me!) through so many difficult situations. I had so much to live for. I decided that my big, fat, beautiful ass was not an apology or an embarrassment or something shameful—it was a gift! Just as a brain cyst that no one would ever wish for was a catalyst for change in my life, my big fat ass had taught me something invaluable. Empathy. Compassion. For all the teasing, bullying, criticism, and shaming I'd received on behalf of my big ass (and all the self-shaming I'd done), I knew I would never treat another person that way. I decided to be grateful for those experiences, as hurtful as they were.

At this point, I knew I didn't need to "fit," but I did need to survive.

I often tell my clients about this dark moment in my life because, for me, that cyst on my brain was a physical manifestation of an emotional condition I'd been suffering with for most of my life. For so long before I got sick, I'd carried self-esteem issues in my heart. I didn't realize years of repressing my spirit for men who never deserved me in the first place might result in a physical illness. I didn't consider the possibility that absorbing hurtful comments from every direction, shaming myself about my body, and feeling insecure over the parts of me that weren't like everyone else might affect not only my spirit and the inner me but also influence my actual body—the outer me. That cyst on my brain was all my baggage, my body image problems and self-esteem issues. Which is why the decision to do what I did next is so important. I needed to deal with my self-esteem issues *and change my damn story.* I had only one mission: Heal that cyst and in so doing, heal my insecure heart.

I wanted to try to heal naturally, but more radical intervention was needed in order to transition. I was started on diuretics and steroids to reduce the swelling and restore some of my sense of balance. Once things were stabilized, I started researching and trying a wide range of complementary and alternative medical treatments, including chelation therapy, oxygen therapy, intravenous vitamin C, and a green juice detox diet. No more sugar or bread for me. In fact, for a time I went vegan. I needed to cleanse my system and would do whatever was necessary. I wanted to live, and I wanted to be able to take care of my children. I was tired of not being able to walk and having to use my arms to lift my leg when I needed to climb a stair or get up on a curb. I couldn't continue to go on like that, and I didn't want to live a life in which I was unable to exercise or dance.

Struggling to get better, I spent hours searching through an assortment of books looking for any information I could use to help me heal. But it wasn't just my body. I had overloaded my thoughts and emotions with negativity, anger, and regrets about the past. I wasn't going to be able to recover until I let go of the unhappiness I was carrying in my soul, mind, and spirit. My psyche and inner being were cluttered with the emotional equivalent of toxic junk food. For my mental and physical well-being, I absolutely needed to get rid of all this emotional trash. The first change I needed to make was improving my attitude toward myself.

Do Something Different—Change Your Damn Story!

As I realized in the hospital, I needed to learn to really love myself. I'd been beating myself up for years, so kindness was called for. I had to stop calling myself names just because I wasn't like everyone else. It wasn't about "fitting in," trying to lose weight so others would accept me; it was about being healthy—for myself first and then for my children. I needed to put myself in a position where my dreams had a chance of coming true.

I knew there would be real work to do. I knew self-esteem would not just be handed to me on a platter. I did have to change my eating habits (difficult), get regular exercise (difficult), learn discipline around money (difficult). And I still wanted ultimately to find love. But even before that, I knew I needed to stop taking abuse and demand respect.

And something that I never thought I would say: I needed to realize that MY ASS IS A GIFT.

God created all of us and everything about us. And I am learning to be grateful for everything I am.

We all have the equivalent of my *caderas y nalgas*—my fat ass. We all have something that doesn't fit the ideal—all of us. Even that seemingly perfect woman you see on the television, perfectly sized and perfectly groomed. Even she doesn't feel perfect. In my case,

I absolutely have a large backside. So what? Since the time when I was hospitalized, I've lost more than two hundred pounds. But I still have cellulite. It will never go away. And I still have a big butt, and that's not a bad thing. If I'm truly going to love myself, I can't exclude certain parts. It took me many years to realize the truth that nobody is without so-called flaws, which I prefer to think of now as those things that make us unique, and also bestow unique gifts. For me, my ass taught me empathy and compassion; for you, the thing that makes you different may have something else to teach.

Our physical "imperfections" are what make us interesting and beautiful. Look for any lessons they may hold. Celebrate and love your body; this body belongs to you. Celebrate who you are, and focus on the life you want. The more gratitude you feel, the more good things you will manifest for yourself.

CHAPTER 2

Fight for Your Life

I AM THE OLDEST OF FOUR KIDS; MY BROTHER, JUNIOR, IS three years younger; my sister Priscilla is five years younger; and my sister Lily, the baby, is seven years younger. My early childhood was spent pretty idyllically on our family's ranch—we owned several acres in Southern California, and I remember the joy of coming home from school and hopping on the four-wheelers to ride all over our property.

But that didn't last. In 1987, when I was seven years old, everything changed. The stock market crashed, and the California economy flatlined. My parents' business was construction cleanup, but construction had come to an almost complete halt. My parents lost everything, including our house; they had no choice but to start all over again, moving to a small two-bedroom rental apartment in Las Vegas.

Even at my young age, I knew that our new apartment and neighborhood were humble beginnings. Because we had no furniture, we all slept on sheets spread out on the floor to cover the very old carpeting, which was a peculiar shade of pink—and which I was also apparently allergic to, as it resulted in a rash and an expensive trip to the doctor.

Pops, who I always describe as a visionary with an entrepreneurial spirit, decided Las Vegas was the place to be. How did he know that southern Nevada would soon experience a building boom? That's the kind of thing he always seems to know.

When my mom and dad picked up and moved us all to Las Vegas, no relatives or friends preceded them. They had little money in their pockets, and they didn't know a single solitary soul. I know they missed their relatives and friends back in California. When I was little, cell phones were not a regular part of life, and I remember my mother wanting to talk to the people she left behind, but phone calls cost too much. My dad's goal was to provide a better life for his wife and family, and to do this, both of my parents had to take a major leap of faith. My father started his company the old-fashioned way—by knocking on doors, looking for work. In California, we'd had a small fleet of seven or eight trucks going all the time. But when we moved, the business consisted of my father, mother, and one old truck we were able to keep because it was paid off. Thank God for that one old truck, which Dad took very good care of—maintaining it in top condition—because he knew it was going to feed us! Today the business has several hundred employees and almost as many trucks, but back then, it was months before we could afford any furniture. My parents always taught us to appreciate the simple things in life, and when we all went to Walmart to buy foam to lay on top of the carpeting for sleeping, it was a much-anticipated big deal.

That first Vegas apartment is a distant memory, but I do remember that, besides helping my dad run the business, it seemed as though my mom never stopped scrubbing and cleaning, and my dad was always involved with home improvement projects. Our home was always a priority, and as soon as my parents started making more money, they used at least some of it to create a more comfortable space. By the time we moved two years later, my parents had worked magic to transform the space—the floors were covered in new beige carpeting and my dad had repainted everything white. Mom insisted on replacing the tub, which was so stained that no matter how much bleach she used—and trust me, my mom knows how to use bleach—it wouldn't get clean. While they were doing everything else, my parents also replaced the fridge, stove, sink, and all the kitchen cabinets. My dad retiled the kitchen and bath with sparkling white tiles so that it was the most beautiful apartment in the complex. In return for all my parents' hard work, we received a discount on the rent. After we moved, the building management reclaimed the apartment to be used as a model to entice other renters to move in.

We moved because we needed more space, and I liked our next house, a cute three-bedroom, with a small cottage in the back that was used as an office for the business. But life was not always calm in our culturally mixed neighborhood, and one day—I think I was just ten—our little home was the target of a drive-by shooting. I was terrified when I heard the sound of gunshots coming from outside. When the police got there, they could see where the bullets had penetrated the front of the house. By then, my mom had made some new friends, and we were immediately out of there to stay with them. I can still feel my mother's panic as she scurried to scoop us up and get us into the car. I think my parents went back briefly to get our stuff, but there was no way my mom and dad would let us stay there one more night.

We never were able to figure out whether the shooting was accidental—some kids who had gotten hold of a gun—or intentional, and if intentional, why us? But it didn't matter—my parents were taking no chances. They made sure we found another home in a different neighborhood on the other side of town. Within weeks we were in a new house, and that was where we stayed until I finished high school. The house, which was in a peaceful, friendly neighborhood, had a nice yard and palm trees in front. The best part was that I got to have my very own bedroom with my very own closet. The room had a navy blue carpet, and just about everything else was white. For the first time since our financial reversal, I had my own bed, nightstand, and armoire. I was very excited to have a room. My parents were able to buy the house, so we were no longer renters. The business had also grown so much that they were able to rent separate space for the business, so for the first time, our home was just a home.

My parents' priorities in life have always been very straightforward: faith, family, work, and contribution—this last was very important to them, and we were taught to know that when we are blessed, we need to share. Sharing is a circle that never ends. When you give, you also get, but you have to make sure you have a heart of giving. They taught us that family came first, and I took their priorities as well as their devotion completely for granted. Didn't everybody's workaholic father drop everything to run home and stay there whenever anybody in the house was sick? My dad never left any doubt about what was most important to him. He always made sure that we spent Sundays doing something together as a family, and as soon as my parents' business improved, they carved out a month of every summer and the entire family went on vacation. At first we drove in the family truck, but it wasn't long before my father was able to get an RV. The Mexican beaches, including Cancún, were favorite destinations, and we inevitably ended up driving down along the coast to visit our Mexican relatives. We all loved the miles and miles of Mazatlán beaches; my sisters and I couldn't wait to look at all the silver jewelry for sale and get our hair braided by the local ladies with flying fingers. By the time they were finished, each of our heads was covered in dozens of tight braids, so expertly woven that they lasted for days.

But as devoted as my father was, he was just as strict. So was my mom. There were very well-defined house rules that we were expected to follow. We all had to rise and shine before 5:00 A.M., because, as my parents reminded us often, "the early bird catches the worm." Television time was limited, and there were no phone calls after 8:00 P.M. We were a Mexican American family with traditional values and beliefs. I wasn't allowed to go to parties or sleepovers, and I always knew that I wasn't going to be given permission to cut my hair, wear shorter skirts (I have to say that my dad always said this as, "You are beautiful just the way you are—you don't have to try to look like everyone else."), or talk to boys until I was seventeen. I expected that I would be married young, like my parents, and that I would immediately start a family of my own. It never occurred to me to think in terms of a different kind of life. When I was a child, this kind of goal, this kind of life, sounded good to me.

My mom and dad met in Los Angeles when they were teenagers. At sixteen, Mom had already found work cleaning at a small hotel. It was owned by a woman from Vietnam, who my mom claims changed her life. This woman was so appreciative of my hardworking mother that she gave her a place to live as well as regular promotions. By the time my mom turned eighteen, she was full-time manager at the hotel. My parents met when my seventeen-year-old father came to pick up his sister, who was briefly staying there. At the time, my dad had multiple jobs: He was working as an auto mechanic during the days and at a taco shop at night. He was also beginning to start his own construction cleanup business.

My mother's initial reaction to my dad was lukewarm. When he asked her for a date, she said no. He was tall and cute, and so many girls (and women) liked him that it made her uncomfortable. She worried that he was a "player" who might break her heart. My dad persisted, and she began to see, as she puts it, that her young teenage suitor was a "hardworking good man with a good heart." Finally, he presented an argument she was willing to hear: "Look," he said, "I'm sick of dating, and you are the woman I want in my life. Just give me an opportunity, get to know me." On their first date, he had just enough money to buy a meal for my mom and himself, but there was a young boy there, obviously hungry, hoping for some help. My kindhearted dad couldn't look at him and eat, so he handed his plate to the child. That kind act won my mom's heart.

When they got married, my eighteen-year-old dad and nineteen-year-old mom were both very young but amazingly mature. My parents had a small wedding in front of a justice of the peace. I was born a year later. Their big wedding celebration came twenty-five years later, when they renewed their vows in front of the whole family. My mother wore white, and Dad sported a big cowboy hat; they were both beaming. I was so quiet at that moment. Seeing my parents exchanging vows again after twenty-five years, I knew I could never give up on love.

My Precious *Abuelitas*

My two *abuelitas* were unique, life-affirming women who passed on their attitudes to my parents. Both of them were divorced, which was highly unusual in our culture at their time. Women of their generation were expected to stay married and tolerate all kinds of male behavior. Women were expected to make dinner, not waves. Both of my *abuelitas* fought for their lives and for an independent sense of self.

Outwardly, they were very different, but one was no less wonderful than the other, and I adored them both. My mother's mother, my Abuelita Mercedes, never wanted to come to the United States because she preferred living alone with her animals—chickens, dogs, and birds—which she had no intention of ever leaving. She supported herself by selling eggs and the vegetables she grew. Manzanillo, my grandma's small and very humid Mexican town, had one main street; the beach was on one side of it and a lush jungle on the other. Abuelita was a very tiny woman, no more than five feet tall, with long white hair that was always braided, never loose. When I think of her, the sweet picture that always comes to mind is of her sitting in a chair in the yard, her long braids wrapped around her head, old-school. She is praying and throwing corn to the big and little chicks running around her.

Above all else, my *abuelita,* who respected all religions and people, loved God. Orphaned as a child, she grew up in a convent. The highest spiritual lessons life taught her about love and grace were an integral part of her being. She was an inspirational role model, and I always thought of her as being personally connected to anything that had to do with God's love.

In some ways, Abuelita walked the same story I did. She had three children with different partners. Ultimately she preferred living alone to sharing her life with an unfaithful man, and my mother never really knew her father. Despite all the stresses and traumas, Abuelita didn't seem to be capable of anger. I should interject here that I certainly didn't inherit this part of her disposition. When somebody does something to offend or upset me, a quick, reactive, angry response is my usual comeback. I really have worked to rein in my hot temper. But my grandmother appeared to have been blessed with a sweet and saintly disposition. When you were around her, it was easy to see that her doors were always open to anyone who needed support.

Although she had the old-school demeanor of someone from another century, she was also a wisdom-filled woman who was way ahead of her times. When a man's cheating ways made her unhappy, she asked him to leave. Few women of her generation were prepared to live independent lives. But she did. Abuelita was ninety-eight years old when she died. I loved her very much. Abuelita Mercedes was very simple, spiritual, and happy as she talked to and blessed her flowers—and made gratitude a constant practice. She was not only a beautiful soul but also a very powerful being.

My father's mother, who lived near Los Angeles, was another strong influence, but in a completely different way. Grandma Maria, who we all called Mama, was a hardworking woman who worked two jobs in order to maintain her independence. She was a religious Catholic whose home was decorated with candles, all of which inspired regular prayers. Mama had several other spiritual practices, like regularly using sage to cleanse her surroundings. Like her, I now surround myself with candles, and whenever I take out my sage, I remember spending time with Mama.

Mama was a liberal free spirit who was drawn to the bright lights and big city. I felt very lucky when my parents would allow me to go visit her for several days, or even a week, at a time. Mama had dreams of becoming a famous singer, something she never accomplished, but even so, she would practice and sing her heart out on a daily basis. Her example showed me that it was admirable to fight for your dreams. And practice, practice, practice!

Another early riser, Mama was up and alert at the crack of dawn. She had a dog named Toby, and when I was there, we would start the day by feeding him breakfast—hot dogs and bread. Then we would head for Mama's bedroom; it had a window on each side, and you could always see and hear the chirping birds that congregated on nearby bushes. I remember sitting on the extra-wide bed covered with a fancy burgundy velvet spread, a pad and yellow pencil in my hand while Mama played cassette tapes, usually by the famous Mexican singer Ana Gabriel. My job was to quickly write down the lyrics so Mama could then memorize them.

One of the things I loved best about Mama's house was her large guest closet, where she stored an assortment of fancy and vintage clothes, including boots and bangles and bell-bottoms! My grandma allowed me to try things on, and, unbelievably, *SHE LET ME WEAR MAKEUP!!!* "You can wear it," she would say, "but don't tell your father." She had electric blue mascara as well as this magical lipstick that would change colors after it was applied. I would put everything on my face—rouge, foundation, mascara—drawing in the darkest eyebrows you can imagine. I was a hot mess, but I thought I looked fabulous.

Early Lessons from My Parents

My beautiful mother was (and is) a clean freak—a veritable genius with her vacuum cleaner. Retaining an attitude, as well as the same tendency for super cleanliness that had served her so well in her hotel days, she even worried about footprint marks left on the carpet. I'm not talking about dirt here—just the slight indentations left by clean feet. One of my mother's life mottos is, "Soap is not expensive, so there is no excuse for not using it." And I remember hearing more than once, "Rosie, your room will become your apartment; your apartment will become your home. The way you keep it will be a reflection on you. Show some self-respect, some self-love." She was determined that everything we wore was spotless, starched, and well ironed. Because she likes things crisp as well as clean, she even starched and ironed the sheets. As the oldest daughter in the house, it seemed as though I learned how to iron soon after I learned to walk. My mother, who believes in a lot of high steam along with her starch, carefully taught me how to make sure that all the seams in our clothing were perfectly straight.

But for every time my mother said, "Iron this," my father had his own piece of advice.

"Come listen to this!" he would say, excitedly waving a tape or CD. You see, as focused as my mother is on cleanliness, my father is even more obsessed with personal development and self-empowerment. He was passionate and hungry for growth. He always wanted to be learning because he knew that would make him a better provider for his family. He'd say, "Rosie, I'm investing in myself to give you a better future." For as long as I can remember, self-improvement tapes, books, and seminars have been part of his life, and consequently mine. My father is a completely self-made man, and there is no arguing with his success, and he credits a number of motivational teachers, including Napoleon Hill and Dale Carnegie, for his achievements. But when he talks about Tony Robbins, which he did more often than I liked when I was young, it feels as though he is discussing a favorite relative.

I was introduced to the concepts behind self-improvement and life coaching by my father when I was quite young. I remember him heading off to seminars with motivational speakers and leaders, and he would return home excited, talking about what he had learned and the plans he was making to reach his personal and business goals—which would, of course, have an enormous impact on the family. My mother would listen attentively and share his enthusiasm. Many times he exhorted me to "Invest in yourself" or "Educate yourself," "Master your craft" or "Become a better human being," but, if truth be told, I paid almost zero attention to what he was saying.

That was my dad's thing—not mine. I regret not paying attention then. If I had, my life could have been so different.

I also wish I learned more about my father's journey while I was still a child. I knew my father was a self-made man. He came to this country from Mexico when he was twelve. He didn't graduate from high school, and he was challenged by enormous obstacles—not the least of which were language and absolutely no financial resources beyond what he was able to make each week doing physical labor. My dad, always an incredibly devoted husband and father of four children, married when he was a teenager and was only nineteen when I was born. He worked day and night and sacrificed so much for the family. I never saw my dad take an evening to go "hang out with the guys." We always came first. When my father moved us all to Las Vegas in his old truck, he did so because he wanted his children to have more opportunities. He was determined to succeed, and he did it on his own, ultimately creating a multimillion-dollar company.

Ask my father how he managed to do what he did, and he will credit all the self-improvement tapes he purchased and the motivational seminars he made a regular part of his life. He considered the expense an investment in our family's future. I remember seeing a photograph of my father graduating from a leadership conference he attended. He was wearing a suit and tie, which indicated to me that this was a big deal and something he took seriously. He also credits his belief in his dream to make things better. My mom and dad also taught us to share what we have with people who needed help. "And do it with a good heart." Dad, who was always a man of faith, would say. "The only thing that matters is your heart. The more you have, the more you give." My father's purpose was about making sure that we had more opportunities than he did.

I saw firsthand how all those tapes and seminars changed my father, making him calmer and more self-confident. I saw how what he learned helped him deal with large business challenges. Nonetheless, I would listen to my dad talk about things like self-mastery, and I would turn off. My response was very much a knee-jerk reaction. That's how it often is with parents and kids. I admired my dad, but I didn't really want him telling me what to do or how to do it. In other words, I didn't pay enough attention to his process. I thought my father was successful because he was my larger-than-life dad, not because of anything he was consciously doing or any path he was purposefully following.

It was only when I began to focus on my own goals and what I wanted to do that I realized that my father's achievements didn't come about by accident; he was following a well-thought-out path. Sure, his goals were very different from my goals, but we both wanted health and happiness for ourselves and our families and had big dreams and aspirations for ourselves. It was only when I began to focus on my own goals that his voice from years earlier would pop up in my head. I would remember what he said, and his advice would often click into place at the right time, like puzzle pieces.

"Keep Walking— You Can Always Cry on the Way"

That's one of my father's favorite pieces of advice. My dad is relentless. Whenever he, or anyone in the family, is facing a problem, he doesn't give up, and he doesn't stop searching for answers. There is no time in my dad's worldview for feeling sorry for yourself. "You have to fight for your life," I remember him always saying. "*Deja de llorar!* Don't just sit there and cry! Always be action oriented! That's how you get results—your life is important, and you have to fight for it! It's okay to feel what you are feeling, own it, but keep going."

When things went wrong for me, I became paralyzed. Whenever that happened, my father would immediately start saying things that he hoped would shake me out of my immobility: "Get excited! Get moving! Nobody's going to do it for you!" My dad embodies the term "self-made." He would call me out on my sh*t even when I didn't like it. Sometimes we can't be honest with ourselves and need brutal honesty from another person. We may not like it, but we need to appreciate the people who can give us the truth that will help us grow. My father pushed me to challenge myself. He is successful because he has never given up looking for new and better solutions for crisis-ridden challenges in his life. He doesn't give up. And he wants to be sure that nobody around him gives up either. Faced with a problem involving the well-being of anyone in his family, don't expect soft, sympathetic words from my father. Instead, he turns into a hard-edged, inspired-by-love drill sergeant shouting out instructions: "Let's go! Let's do this!" And yes, "Keep walking—you can always cry on the way."

Over and over again, Dad says the same thing: "Stop complaining and show up for yourself—you have to fight for your life!"

You Have to Fight for Your Life

When my father told me to fight for my life, he wasn't just reminding me to continue breathing and take care of my physical being. He had a much larger and more profound goal in mind. I want you to stop and think about this. Don't just think about all the stuff that's going on around you right now, no matter how large or small it seems at the moment. Think about the bigger picture. Think about your faith and what you believe in; think about what you perceive as your purpose in life. And if you aren't sure about what your purpose is, think about it long and hard until you start to figure it out. If money were not an issue, what would you want to do with your life? What would it look like? What would it feel like? What sets your soul on fire? As my father often reminded me, "You don't want to find yourself at the end of your life filled with regrets because you never took a chance and fought for what you believed in." Growing up, I couldn't help but be aware that both of my parents were strong believers in fighting for what is right as well as for their lives—an attitude that was instilled in them by my two *abuelitas*, both of whom fought to maintain their authenticity as well as their values. Have the fearlessness to ask for what you want. Let the universe know that you are ready. The key is learning to ask with clarity. Always remember: The universe is listening.

My dad is fifty-nine and still as driven as he was when he was young. In his life, I believe he attracted more abundance because he was always value-driven rather than ego-driven. A huge, energetic change takes place in your life when you put your values first. My dad's primary purpose was making sure that his children had more opportunities than he did. When I was younger, I craved attention as well as money. Now I realize that I am primarily concerned with leaving a future legacy for my children. That's what matters.

Start living by your purpose and don't worry about p*ssing some people off along the way. If you want to lead your best life, you can't always wait for other people's validation. Remind yourself that fighting for your life means embracing your authentic self. Life is about discovering who you are and making a statement by what you say and how you act. Every day, when you get out of bed, tell yourself, MY LIFE MATTERS! I MATTER! This is a powerful statement. Never stop fighting for your dreams. Go create—and claim what is yours!

CHAPTER 3

Your Voice Matters

IF YOU LOOK AT MY PHOTO ALBUMS FROM MY HIGH SCHOOL years, you won't find a single photograph of me going to a prom, dance, or ball game. I suffered from an all-pervasive sense of not belonging and can honestly say that I didn't attend even one school social event. I struggled to make myself invisible and never spoke up; few of my classmates even knew my name. The kinder ones, who used a friendly nickname, might have called out to me, "Hi, doll-face." Others called me "hippo," "fat ass," or worse.

While at home with my family, I knew I was loved and had a place where I belonged. At school, even when things appeared to be going okay, I was on alert, expecting someone to do or say something hurtful; I felt like an alienated stranger who was about to be harassed or abused. Looking back, I realize that this was something I had to experience to become the person I was meant to be. Back then, I was primarily connected to my discomfort.

It goes without saying that I allowed my weight to play a key role in my unhappiness. From my admittedly distorted point of view, it seemed as though my classmates were getting thinner and thinner while I was growing larger and larger. I know now that this was all in my mind, but then, there was never a moment when I didn't think that I was huge compared to other girls, and every plus-size pound weighed as heavily on my psyche as it did on my hips. Was I destined always to be defined by my size?

My mom is a great cook. Our day began with a large, wonderful breakfast that included ham, eggs, refried beans, and sweet Mexican bread with cinnamon—perfect for dipping into amazing dark coffee with sweet cream. It is so light and delicious that it's almost impossible not to devour it, which I did—daily. Although I totally loved to eat, my cooking skills are mediocre. My mother taught me how to clean, but her lessons about cooking never really took. I *can* cook, but I didn't need to because my mother was a superwoman—she did it all.

My parents, who stressed learning, always wanted to make sure that we had a good education in a safe environment, so soon after arriving in Vegas, they pulled together enough money to send me to a private Catholic school, where I was one of only a few Mexican American girls. This reinforced my sense of being different from the other girls, who bonded together in cliques. I was always on the sidelines and always alone.

We had regular teachers, not nuns, but there was still a lot of praying. The school was run by a priest whose previous experience had been as a priest in a jail; maybe that was his excuse for treating the students as though they were inmates. During choir practice, he was particularly obsessed with making sure that we were all singing as loudly as possible. I remember standing there for what seemed like hours, all of us screaming louder and louder until he was satisfied.

I think every girl who ever went to a Catholic school has complained about "the uniform." Mine was no different: Girls had to wear ugly cotton T-shirts tucked into our uglier navy blue pleated skirts. As the heaviest girl in the class, I was known as the girl with the pretty face and big butt. Those skirts made even skinny girls look overweight, so of course they made my ample hips look even larger than they were. I would try to cover up as much as possible, wrapping myself in oversize sweaters even when the Las Vegas temperatures were well over a hundred. And yes, at that time, my weight and Latina heritage made me an obvious target for bullying. It was brutal. During PE, some of the other girls would try to hit me with the volleyball. I remember one screaming, "Move it because you can't run, fatso!" Everything about me set me apart from the other girls, and, although not everybody in school was mean, I had no friends or defenders and felt isolated and worried about what was going to happen next.

In one of my first body-shaming incidents, I remember going down the metal slide on the school playground. Some kids started throwing rocks at me. When the rocks hit the slide, there was a loud thunk! Thunk! Thunk! Thunk! It felt like an earthquake. I loved going down that slide, but after that experience, I don't think I ever again got on it. Like ostracized kids everywhere, I quickly developed my own system of dealing with recess. I simply separated from the group and went off to sit on the side or play tetherball by myself.

Although I was heavy, I was actually quite athletic, and people remember me as a tomboy, hanging out with my brother and his friends, climbing trees. As kids, my brother, Junior, and I had a classic boy/girl sibling relationship. We were always together—and always arguing. I inevitably wanted the opposite of what he wanted, and vice versa. My sensitive mother, who perhaps might have preferred a more feminine daughter, encouraged my creative side. She managed to track down a retired art teacher neighbor, who agreed to give me lessons. After school, three days a week, I went to her house, where I learned to paint, draw, and do various arts and crafts. Now, when I design a piece of clothing or jewelry, I look back to those afternoons. They gave me skills and confidence, as well as an early understanding about how to approach creative projects.

My life at school became even more difficult when I reached those preteen years when boys and girls start noticing one another. I must have been just starting seventh grade when some of the meanest girls decided that they would write a note to the cutest and most popular boy in the class telling him how admired and desired he was—signing it with my name. I saw what they were doing, but I couldn't stop them. It's impossible to forget the expression on his face when he read the note and saw the signature. I was so upset that I managed to convince my mother that I was sick and stayed out of school for the rest of the week. I was beyond humiliated, and if I had my way, I never would have returned.

Finding Satisfaction

I was a sophomore when one of my mom's friends won tickets to an event at the local Spanish radio station and took me with her.

The on-air hosts started directing questions to audience members, and I found they kept coming back again and again to me. When I asked questions, responded, or answered, people laughed. They asked me more questions. I answered back. And I giggled. People laughed even harder. They liked me. One of the announcers asked me to come back again. I was thrilled, but as a girl who'd always tried to disappear in public, I was also nervous. I was accustomed to people laughing at me, not with me. This was such a different experience, and I loved everything about it. In many ways, my second visit was a repeat of the first. And, once again, they asked me to come back.

Given what my life was like as an insecure fifteen-year-old teenager, ending up on the radio was truly an example of life and the universe redirecting me. Before long, I was a regular at the station for the early-morning show, happy just to show up and do whatever they asked. I was the funny, laughing teenager who felt accepted and quickly caught on to what I was meant to be doing. I also think the strong work ethic that my parents ingrained in me from birth took hold. I loved what I was doing and wanted to do a good job. Before I turned sixteen and got my driver's license, my mother drove me to the station in the morning; she would bring home-brewed Mexican coffee for everybody—something that immediately improved my popularity with everyone there. I started as an unpaid volunteer and intern, but within a few months, I was getting a real paycheck. Yes, it was minimum wage, but it felt like a small fortune to me.

The main on-air personality was Chava Gomez, who was a favorite Spanish radio personality. He was an amazing mentor—a kind and encouraging guy who taught me so much, particularly how to think on my feet. I learned an important radio rule: No matter what, there should never be any "dead air"—more than a moment when nobody is speaking. Not only did Chava and the other great co-host, Angel Maciel, who is now in Colorado, teach me how to use my voice and vary my tone; they also helped me perfect my Spanish, which was so sloppy at the time that the main DJ got phone calls complaining that I didn't sound authentic. It was downright embarrassing, and I knew I had to do better and spent long hours working on my accent.

When Angel gave me instructions about my diction, I felt a little like Eliza Doolittle being educated by Professor Higgins. I will always remember some of his early lessons about being on-air. "Be still," he told me, "and just let your thoughts flow. Don't be afraid to speak up and speak out. When something goes wrong, improvise. And be passionate!" From doing radio, I learned how to accept thoughts coming through my head and then quickly release them out of my mouth without getting nervous or censoring myself.

Finding My Voice

I didn't start out in life expecting to have a media presence. But for some reason, I was comfortable being on-air. I sometimes think back about my frame of mind at the time. Why was I—the girl who was over-the-top anxious about walking into school every day—able to talk freely before a large radio audience? Obviously the fact that the audience couldn't see me made a huge difference. I knew I was not going to be judged by my weight, which felt liberating. At school, I was still the girl with the fat ass trying not to be noticed—still so nervous about being noticed that I didn't even want to go to the school cafeteria and spent hours hiding out in the ladies' room. At the radio station, however, where I was encouraged to speak up and speak out, I was fearless about being heard. I started to find my voice and, on-air at least, became the real me. Having a job and going to work saved me. It showed me that taking risks could pay off.

At the station, I developed a very clear set of duties. I was there initially to be a sidekick and provide amusing small talk with the hosts in between the music from the *Billboard* Latino Hot 100 that the station was famous for playing. But within a short time, I graduated to doing weather and traffic. The people working there made me feel as though I was worthy and had a talent. They always referred to me as "the girl with the pretty face." This was so much better than being known as the girl with the big butt! What teenage girl with image issues wouldn't love being introduced in this way? I felt a little happier every time I heard it said.

ANNOUNCER: So what's going on with the roads out there today? Here's the girl with the pretty face to give us a heads-up.

ME: Right now it's light sweater weather with a temperature of fifty-nine chilly desert degrees in the beautiful Vegas valley, but expect it to rise up to the mid-seventies by noon. And if you are out there driving right now, there is a small accident at Las Vegas Boulevard and Tropicana, so you might want to avoid the Boulevard. Try I-15 instead.

Every morning, when I walked into that gray radio studio with the soundproof windows and the blinking sign, I felt a little thrill go through me. On-air, you have to learn to think on your feet and respond. As I learned how to handle calls, I was also learning how to be comfortable in my own skin. We spent a fair amount of time every morning answering call-ins and doing shout-outs. I really loved seeing the dashboard fill up with lights because people were calling, proof that somebody was listening and paying attention to what we were saying. That's when I really recognized that *my voice matters.*

RICARDO, A CALLER FROM GREEN VALLEY: Am I really on the radio? I want to wish my wife, Ana, a happy birthday. She turns forty-two today. Can I say I love you to my wife?

ME: You sure can! And happy birthday, Ana! Ricardo, did you get your wife a special present for her birthday? Stay on the phone, and get a free pair of tickets for this week's concert. Ana will love this!

And, here's a special shout-out to all the people working at the casinos and all those great men and women working construction around them. What radio station does it best? Turn it up and get ready to party!

One of my favorite segments every morning was our daily prank. Listeners would call in and ask us to prank somebody. I will never forget Maria, who asked us to call her boyfriend, José, and tell him that Maria was pregnant, which of course she wasn't. I played the nurse from the doctor's office.

ME: José, is that you?

JOSÉ: Yes.

ME: Good morning, José, I'm calling from the Vegas Medical Clinic with some great news! Your wife, Maria, was here yesterday, and we wanted to share the news that the test is positive.

JOSÉ: Maria isn't my wife. We're not married. What test?

ME: The pregnancy test.

JOSÉ: What pregnancy test?! What do you mean, "positive"? There must be some mistake. We're not married. We always used protection. This is a mistake!

To this day, I wonder whether the relationship between Maria and José survived that prank.

In less than a year, my role at the station expanded and I started doing entertainment news and gossip. I spent more time doing research for my entertainment news segment than I did for any school report or math homework. By the time I was a senior, I was also doing red-carpet interviews in Vegas. Depending on which performers were in town, I would head off late on Friday or Saturday nights, followed by my tech crew, to talk to Latino celebrities at a variety of events, mostly at the hotels after the shows. Because it was radio, I didn't have to think twice about my hips being seen. I even got to interview my biggest teenage crush and idol, Alejandro Fernández. I still remember preparing for the interview and writing down and memorizing a whole bunch of questions about his latest single and how he liked being in Vegas. I was getting my feet wet and learning the basics about the entertainment business.

Looking back now, my life was definitely split in two. One minute, I would be out working on Saturday night, like an adult, with a crew and doing celebrity interviews, but when I got home, I would dutifully slip into my role as the carefully watched teenage daughter who wasn't allowed to make or receive phone calls after 8:00 P.M. That said, from day one my parents completely supported my developing dream. My dream was different from theirs; maybe they didn't understand what I was doing, but they were 100 percent behind me and excited for me. I thought it was the coolest thing when they'd tell their employees to tune in and listen to me.

My weekday schedule was not that of your typical teenager. I was in bed and asleep every night by 9:00 P.M.—then up at 2:00 A.M. so I could get ready and drive to the station, where I would go on the air at 3:00 A.M. and stay there until 7:00 A.M. My mornings were more than hectic. School started at 7:30, but by the time I arrived for class, it was usually closer to 8:00, or even later. For the most part, my teachers were very forgiving and made allowances. Some even commended me for my work ethic. But, truth be told, many mornings I fell asleep during those first classes and then dozed my way through the rest of the day without always being aware of what was going on. I loved some classes, like science. Others I primarily focused on trying to stay awake.

My biggest nightmare took place during my 1:15 P.M. gym class.

The stalls had no doors, so there was absolutely no privacy when getting dressed. I had a way of slithering in and out of my clothes, making sure I was always covered. As uncomfortable as it was, I wore my PE shorts under my skirt. I would look at the other girls walking around in their thongs and envy their bodies. Even at my age, I had cellulite. *Seventeen* magazine, which I read religiously every month, never said anything about cellulite.

And then, of course, the bullying continued. Adding to my sense of leading a double life was the fact that few of my fellow students had any idea that I had morphed into a minor radio celebrity. I was working on a Spanish language radio station, and hardly any of my fellow students were Spanish speaking. This was not a station they turned on. One day as school was getting out, I remember calmly starting to walk to my car so I could drive home. I was in a relatively cheerful mood, but out of the blue, three typical jock-type guys began pointing at me and making comments about my hips. The confrontation was so sudden that I felt as though I had been slapped. My sense of humiliation was overwhelming, followed almost immediately by a waterfall of tears. I started running. As I did, the school security guard, who patrolled the grounds on his bicycle, rode over and stopped me. He obviously listened to my radio station. "You just stop running," he said. "Don't let those a**holes run you off! I never want to see you running away like that. Remember, you're working on the radio. You're doing so much more than just going to high school. They're not doing sh*t!" From that day forward, whenever he saw me, he would walk me to my car. I loved and will never forget that guy, who turned into one of my high school heroes.

During those years, I began to realize that I wasn't the only teenage girl with body issues. A particularly confusing high school memory involves a conversation I overheard. I was in a stall in the ladies' room, hiding out, trying my best not to provide a target for some of the mean girls. Several of these girls entered the space, not realizing I was there and could hear them. One of the skinniest girls in the group told the others that she was accustomed to her mother finding fault with her body and calling her "Jell-O thighs"! The girl said that she solved her problems with weight by sticking her finger down her throat and throwing up whenever she ate anything "fattening." Hearing her tell her friends about the times that her mother pinched her fat, I remember thinking, *She has no fat to pinch.* I was so shocked. I just thought she was the most beautiful girl in the world. She was gorgeous and fit. I was only just beginning to be aware of the image issues that so many women share no matter what their size or ethnic background. I recently saw a quote that said, "Men think it's every girl's dream to find the perfect man. Not true! What girls really dream about is being able to do whatever the hell they want without being judged—and eating anything they want without gaining a pound." I couldn't help laughing. So much emphasis is put on size and body type that there are very few women who have not been made to feel insecure about how they look.

As a teenager, I really was like two extremely different girls. In my personal life with others at school, I was quiet and isolated and insecure because of my weight and the ongoing rejection I got from my peers. I was only one of two girls in my school who were really plus-size. Everyone else was a 2 or a 4, or so it seemed to me.

I had nobody to look to as some kind of role model. When classmates insulted me, I was totally afraid of expressing myself, let alone standing up for myself. I was the girl walking next to the wall, hugging my books and looking down at the floor.

But in my work life, whether it was doing makeup or having a job in radio, I was unusually fearless and bold. I was proud of my ability to do this. When I was on the radio, I was amazingly capable of responding, speaking out, and saying whatever came into my mind.

Self-discovery is important no matter how old you are, but learning more about who you are and what you want from life is highlighted during your teen years. Lurking in each of us is an insecure adolescent psyche with dreams both of belonging and of standing out in some way. We always need to protect and encourage that part of ourselves—that's the part of us that has something important to say.

Your Voice Matters

Speak your mind! Let others know what is going on in your busy head. Share your ideas, and try to make the world a better place. We each have a mission, and our voices tell the story.

When I was on the radio, I was sometimes anxious and not everything came out perfectly. But I couldn't worry about what others were going to think. Don't ever let the opinions of others paralyze you. Their opinion is powerless—it doesn't matter—and your voice is powerful.

When you feel anxiety coming up, repeat to yourself: *My voice matters.* Take a few deep breaths and affirm yourself. Say it again: *My voice matters.* This is a powerful habit to create in your life. Speak to yourself slowly and firmly. And don't be apologetic about it.

Like the eyes, your voice is a window to your soul. And it starts with speaking up. Don't be afraid to ask for what you want. Don't be afraid to say yes, and don't be afraid to say no. And don't be afraid to stand up for yourself.

Tell yourself once again: *As long as I'm breathing, my feelings are valid and my voice is powerful. My voice matters.*

CHAPTER 4

Just Keep

LATINOS HAVE A CULTURAL AS WELL AS RELIGIOUS TRADITION known as a Quinceañera. This event, which marks the time when a young girl turns fifteen, celebrates her journey from childhood to feminine maturity. A Quinceañera celebration typically includes a religious ceremony as well as a reception or party for family and friends. It's a very exciting time. True to tradition, my family-oriented parents decided they were going to go all out and throw a huge party after the religious ceremony in the church. All out! I'm talking about inviting several hundred people. It would be a huge event, bringing together as many family members and friends as possible. I would get to wear a beautiful white ball gown, along with a crown of flowers. And, for the very first time, I would also wear high heels.

Two important things happened while I was preparing for my Quinceañera. One: I made a friend at school—the other plus-size girl. Genesis had long, curly, flowing hair, beautiful eyes, a wonderful smile, and a great sense of humor. I was so happy to have somebody to talk to. Not only did Genesis make me laugh, she made me feel as though I had a real friend who understood me. She never judged me, and I could be myself around her. Like me, Genesis was Mexican American. But her parents were significantly more relaxed than mine, and she was given much more freedom. I remember envying her because she was allowed to go to parties and, even more important, she also got invited to them. We first bonded over our shared body issues, and slowly but surely we developed a strong friendship. I was so happy that she became a part of my life. I had a friend to talk to and laugh with, and this was a great thing.

The other important addition to my life was the man whose support and kindness altered my entire view of the world. My mom is the kind of supermom who notices everything. Yes, she sees the slightest bit of dirt or the smallest crumb left behind on a table, but she also always notices how her children are feeling. Even though she didn't talk about it, she was hypersensitive to my unhappiness and was diligently on the lookout for ways to improve my life. You could almost hear her brain whirling as she tried to find ways to make me feel better about myself. That's how Carlos entered my world. My mom had heard through the grapevine that there was a Spanish-speaking hair stylist and makeup expert in town; he had done makeovers on tons of models, as well as Miss Universe contestants. Good news! With luck, he might be able to help prepare her insecure daughter for her Quinceañera.

Carlos had been born in Veracruz, and before I even met him, I heard a little bit about his exotic background. Before becoming a Las Vegas stylist, makeup artist, and beauty expert, he had been a world-traveled dancer. When we met, Carlos, a tall, graceful man with incredible green eyes, was already in his sixties; I thought he was the best-looking older man I had ever seen. For his part, Carlos took one look at me and immediately realized that I was in dire need of a lot of help and confidence building. At one time, Carlos had been married to another dancer with whom he had a child—a daughter he had raised. I always felt that Carlos took a strong paternal interest in me because he missed his daughter, now grown and raising a family of her own.

On a large-scale philosophical level, Carlos taught me the importance of learning to move with life. "Just dance," he would say. I would nod, understanding that Carlos was advising me about how to live a happier life. But on a much more practical level, Carlos was also expected to teach me how to dance in high heels, something I would be expected to do for my Quinceañera celebration. Let me start by saying, I was a sneakers kind of girl. I have big—okay, huge—feet. Size 11. Almost as soon as I arrived at Carlos's home for my first dancing lesson, he pulled out these beautiful designer heels. I put them on and gave it a try. The first thing I did was fall. The second thing I did was fall again. Finally I was able to stand in them, but I was listing to one side and was about to fall again when Carlos took over. "Here," he said. "Let me show you. If I can do it, you can do it." He put on heels and started gracefully walking all over the place. I'd never seen a man in heels before. He looked beautiful, but he still made me laugh. I was so comfortable with Carlos. It was okay to make mistakes and it was okay to laugh about them. A couple of more falls and a lot of laughs, and I thought I had some idea about what to do. By the second lesson, Carlos was teaching me how to dance. We started with the waltz, but we eventually progressed to flamenco. I loved it more than I can describe. "Get excited and start dancing. Dancing even heals heartbreak," Carlos told me as we joyfully spun around the room.

Carlos changed my view of the world. He was fluent in Spanish, English, and French, and he also spoke some Italian. Listening to his stories of traveling through Europe and living in Paris and Milan opened my eyes to possibilities that existed beyond Las Vegas, Nevada—and altered my aspirations. Some of his lessons were simple but valuable. He taught me how to stop flinging myself across chairs and sit up straight with my legs crossed at the ankle. He also took me out to good restaurants, teaching me how to order and which fork to use for what. He would punctuate our conversations with bits of advice about life, manners, and protocol. "A true lady doesn't put herself or anyone else down," he told me. I should also mention that what Carlos knew better than anyone was makeup. I didn't realize it at the time, but Carlos's lessons provided the groundwork for what would turn out to be the career that would support me and my children for many years.

Before I met Carlos, it never occurred to me that anyone would consider me pretty enough to want to take my picture. I knew nothing about the magic that hair products and makeup could create. I knew how to brush out my hair, but as far as trying to make myself look more attractive and presentable, getting the snarls out of my hair was about it. I will always remember the first time Carlos cut my hair and did my first makeover.

There I was, sitting in his chair at the salon, and I was in serious agony trying not to complain, cry, or even say "ouch." Carlos, who had a pair of tweezers in his hand, was slowly and carefully plucking away at the hairs growing across the top of my nose. No question but that I was growing a serious and very unattractive unibrow. From the determined expression on his face I could see the amount of energy that Carlos was prepared to spend to make this facial hair disappear.

"Always pluck," he told me. "Never, ever wax!"

This was probably the first advice that Carlos ever gave me, and I will never forget it, because Carlos carefully explained that I needed to take care of my appearance as though I really, really mattered. "Treat yourself with the care you deserve. Don't rush. Plucking takes time and thought. Taking good care of yourself is a form of self-respect."

Carlos shared a beauty tip a minute and spoke with such authority that his advice left a lifelong imprint on my brain. "Always pluck. Never, ever wax!" I remember repeating to myself. At that point in my life, I couldn't imagine that I would ever be doing any plucking or waxing, but nonetheless he sounded so convincing that I paid careful attention to his words.

When Carlos was finally satisfied with my brows, he took out a small clean silver spoon and used it to very gently curl my eyelashes. A silver spoon! Where did he learn to do that? I wondered if I would ever be able to do that for myself.

Carlos had already cut and shaped my hair, leaving it long but adding layers that gave it body and shape. When he was finished with his work, he twirled my chair around in a dramatic gesture, and I got my first real look at myself. I was amazed. I looked like a different person. How was this possible? Could this girl with the beautifully shaped eyebrows and shiny hair really be me?

"You look beautiful," Carlos told me, and for at least a few minutes, I believed him. Other people had told me that I had a pretty face, but I didn't really believe them. I thought they were being kind to me because I was so fat. My mom said nice things to me. But I certainly didn't believe her because she was my mom, who loved me. With Carlos, I felt the very small beginnings of self-confidence. This was a benchmark in my life. I actually started to believe what Carlos had told me and started making it my truth, that I was beautiful.

A Different Way of Looking at Myself

Before Carlos, I thought of myself as a tomboy. I had no interest in makeup or beauty tips. I didn't think that I could ever look pretty, so why even try? Modeling was not remotely one of my childhood goals. I don't think I ever knew what a model was or did.

Carlos changed all that. He introduced me to a world that included not only beauty magazines and makeup but also fashion. Because of his guidance, I became interested in things that helped me create and shape a career.

I can never forget the first time Carlos took me shopping. He told me that he wanted to buy me my very own makeup kit, and we headed to a store with a large makeup department.

"Remember," he advised, "you are protecting your skin for a lifetime, so always buy the best you can."

When it came to brands of makeup, Carlos definitely had his favorites. I watched him sort through a variety of foundation makeup in different shades before settling on one with a truly astonishing price tag. "This one is good," he said, gesturing to the salesperson, who nodded in agreement.

After we left the store, we went out for coffee. As I watched and listened, Carlos spread out our purchases, explaining why he chose each one. It was amazing. I was now the proud owner of an impressive assortment of foundations, shadows, bronzers, and glosses. He told me which shadows would be appropriate for evening wear when I might want what he called "smoky eyes" and which ones to use during daylight hours. As we packed everything up, I was so looking forward to getting back home, where I would be able to sit in front of a mirror and practice.

The Reason People Enter Our Lives

Here's the most important takeaway from meeting Carlos when I did: I learned that God sends people into our lives for a reason. There is always a lesson in everything that happens to us, and there is always a blessing. The thing to remember is that no matter how dark the season feels, some light is always peeking through. If we pay attention to what is going on around us, we learn to realize and notice why people enter our lives when they do. I didn't always understand everything Carlos was trying to teach me, but I always knew it was important.

Carlos's first lessons helped me learn something extremely important: **Being Different Is Never a Bad Thing.** This is something we all need to appreciate. Recognize that your differences represent an original "You" thing! Life has taught me that there is beauty to be found in every stage and in all the ups and downs of your life. Look for the positive in every situation. Even when you think you are hiding from the world, the universe is sending you people and experiences that can help you see the beauty in your own life. When you least expect it, you are being shown the good things about yourself that you may not even be aware exist.

Carlos was such a positive force for me. Whenever possible, I would run off to spend time at his salon. Even when he had customers, he was always welcoming and smiled when he saw my face. I liked to sit there and read fashion or beauty magazines. Sometimes if he wasn't busy, he would sit and talk with me about the articles and the beauty tips. Our school had a custom—Ditch Day. All the kids would skip school with their friends and do whatever they wanted. I remember one Ditch Day when I was particularly upset because several boys had broken into my locker, grabbing my books and saying mean things to me. I was so happy to be with Carlos, where I felt safe and protected. After he was finished with his client, Carlos washed my hair and blew it dry. "This is a beautiful blowout," he said, "but what really matters is the beauty you carry within yourself. Nobody can take that away from you. If anybody ever says negative things to you, don't believe what they are saying. That is not your truth." Carlos was more than just a great teacher. He was an important male figure in my life. On the day of my Quinceañera, Carlos made the crown of flowers I wore on my head. I miss him. I miss his energy and his contagious laugh. Whenever Carlos laughed, I couldn't help but laugh with him.

Starting My Own Makeup Business

As a teenager, my radio job wasn't my only source of income. When I ran off to visit Carlos, I received a great deal of comfort and support, but I was also getting lessons in creating magic with cosmetics. I reinforced that by doing a great deal of research reading the current books and magazines that featured information about makeup application and techniques. I guess at least in part, I was trying to bolster my self-image by focusing on my face and not my body.

Sometimes I would bring my makeup kit to school with me, and during lunch hour, my friend Genesis and I would sit at a table in the yard, and I would do her face and her eyes, using all the tricks of the trade that I had learned from Carlos. Genesis and I would invariably have our favorite magazines with us so we could try the newest makeup ideas. Genesis, who was very colorful, loved the idea of wearing the newest trend. If a current fashion magazine featured a model wearing blue neon on her face, she was absolutely up for it! Other girls would sometimes wander over and stand there to watch what I was doing. I still remember a girl watching us and asking me the magic question, "How much would you charge to do my makeup?"

I hesitated one nanosecond before answering, "Twenty-five dollars." I wanted to sound secure and confident, so I made a point of barely looking up from what I was doing.

"Oh my God," Genesis said as soon as the other girls walked away, "you are going to make so much money!"

I sure hoped she was right.

Before long, I was the school's go-to makeup person. If there was any kind of prom or dance, girls would line up to make sure I would be available. I even began getting calls about other events, like weddings. I didn't question it at the time, but in retrospect I realize that it was amazing how my name started getting out more and more;

sometimes my pager wouldn't quit, and there were many weekends when I was booked solid.

Eventually I developed a system for major school events: The girls would arrive at my house, carrying their dresses, with their skin clean, moisturized, and prepped, per my instructions. They would lay their dresses out on the bed, strip down to their underwear, and I would get to work on their faces. I even had a small assistant—my little sister Lily, now an amazing hair stylist and makeup artist—who would watch what I was doing. At the time, it didn't even occur to me that she was learning things that she would later use to establish her own career. I followed the routines I learned from Carlos. I used real art brushes and sponges that I bought at an art supply store and sanitized in between each use. As much as I tried to emulate Carlos, I was never able to learn his technique of curling eyelashes with a silver spoon. I tried and tried, but I could never do it.

No matter what was going on in my life, I stayed close to Carlos, who was very proud that he had contributed to my ability to earn a living. In the middle of my senior year, my family went to Mexico for the Christmas holidays, and as always, I phoned Carlos to wish him a Merry Christmas and Happy New Year. He didn't answer; he also didn't answer the next day, or the next. Finally, after about four days of calling, someone picked up his phone. It was his daughter. She gave me the sad news. Carlos, who had suffered from diabetes for years, had experienced a major health crisis and died. This was a huge loss and one that continues to fill me with great sadness. However, I often feel that he is sending me messages in spirit. There is not a day that goes by without my thinking about him and remembering his signing off conversations by saying, *"Bisoux." Kisses.*

Taking Carlos's Techniques with Me

Every time I did someone's makeup, I started with a hydrating spritz, which I would let dry before applying a hydrating cream and foundation in the right shade for the girl's skin as well as the time of day. I used concealer to hide blemishes and under-eye circles. Then I contoured the girl's face, using a variety of bronzers, powders, and other products. It's amazing the effect contouring can have in changing the appearance of the shape of someone's nose. And, of course, I always used eye shadow. Throughout I took the time to blend carefully. Carlos always said, "Blend, blend, blend—you can never spend too much time blending." I accented the eyes with eyeliner before gluing on eyelashes, Finally, I would use lip liner and fill in the lips using different products depending on whether the girl wanted a matte or glossy look.

I even developed my own shimmer that I would use on their legs, arms, and chest to give them a healthy glow. I still remember the first time one of the girls gave me a tip. It was an extra $5, and I didn't understand why she was giving it to me.

"It's a tip," she said. "Haven't you ever had your makeup done?"

"Yes, lots," I told her. "But only by one person, and he doesn't charge me."

If there was a really big event taking place, I would start working on girls Saturday morning. My handiwork would often have to last until evening, so I was very careful about how it was applied.

The first Saturday that I did makeup for an event, I ended up with $200. By the time I graduated, there were many weekends that I earned well over $1,000 and girls—even some who had talked sh*t about my weight in school—would arrive in shifts, expecting me to work magic. It was nice to be recognized at school for something besides the size of my hips.

Financially, as a teenager, I was doing better than okay. Between the money I made at the radio station and my work with makeup, I managed to save a hefty little nest egg. I opened my own bank account, and I loved watching my money grow. My father, the entrepreneur to end all entrepreneurs, was pretty proud of me.

Start Dancing

Carlos gave me the courage to dance, to move and duck and weave in and out of sometimes complicated situations. Dance is more than movement; it's a statement to the world that you're comfortable being exactly who you are. "Get excited and start dancing. Allow your spirit to be free," he would tell me. Yes, of course, I thought to myself, realizing for the first time that I didn't have to hide; I could get up on the floor where people could see me and let my heart out. I was seen, and it was an amazing emotional experience.

Feeling defeated? Keep dancing.

Having a bad day? Put on some music and start moving your body.

Feeling stuck? Think about ways to gracefully get yourself to a different situation, one step at a time.

Feeling self-conscious? Don't. Instead, set your spirit free.

You can change your emotional state in the snap of a finger. The question is, do you want to? It's your own personal choice to stay where you are or change your emotional state. Get excited, choose to be happy, always come from gratitude—whether an experience is good or bad—and dance your ass off. Whether an experience is positive or negative is determined by the spin you give it. What's done is done. It's your choice: Do you want to stay stuck thinking about what happened and the emotions that were attached to the experience? Or do you want to let go and move on? Why not start changing today? Create a new mental vision and new emotions. All you have is the present moment. This is your life. Create something new and something different. Get excited. Say, *F*ck yeah, it's my time.* Enjoy it! It belongs only to you.

Opportunity dances with those who are already on the dance floor. Get up and start creating the momentum you need. Start creating your opportunity.

CHAPTER 5

Your First Chance Isn't Your Last Chance

LET ME BE HONEST ABOUT SOMETHING: I KNOW WHAT IT IS to have an unfortunate romantic history. You were going to figure that out anyway, so let's just get it out of the way now.

As a teenager, I was establishing ideas about relationships that wouldn't serve me well. My problems may have started with all the name-calling and bullying I experienced as a child. I really didn't believe anyone would ever find me attractive or desirable. Of course, just like anyone else who breathes and has a pulse, I desperately hoped that somebody would fall in love with me, but I didn't expect it was going to happen in the way that it did. I had a different movie playing in my head. Something more like my parents' relationship. When a boy paid attention to me, my first reaction was shock. Then I had a series of truly stupid thoughts somewhere along the lines of "He seems to like me. No boy may ever like me again, so I had better do everything possible to make sure he sticks around, because this may be my last and only chance at love."

The "he may be my last chance" reaction is common among women with troubled self-esteem. A girl or woman, no matter what her age, who is more secure and confident looks at the guy who is paying attention to her and thinks, "He seems okay, but let me learn more about him. Do we have similar interests and values? Is he a reliable, honest, moral person with whom I genuinely want to share an evening, let alone a life? Let me take my time and figure out if this is the right person for me. If he is not, I'm desirable and worthy, and there are lots of people who will want to be with me." If you have never said this out loud, here is an opportunity to say it loud and clear: ***I'm desirable and worthy and there are lots of people who will want to know me and spend quality time with me. The right person will fall in love with me and stay in love with me for the right reasons.***

I know all that now, but as a young person just starting to be aware of romantic possibilities, I hadn't figured much of it out. I had such a longing to be loved. And like many other young people, I didn't know enough to hold back my emotions and take it slow.

My first real crush was a boy named Gilbert. I actually thought, *He is perfect.* I was sixteen; he was twenty and worked for my father doing construction cleanup. My reasons for liking him were simple and straightforward: He paid attention to me; he was sweet; he laughed a lot; and, as a five-nine girl, I loved that he was also tall—six foot four.

He started coming over in the evening during the summer before my junior year. As first loves go, this one was serious. Gilbert, who understood and respected my parents' old-school values, actually asked my father for permission to court me. My dad didn't let me go out on dates, but three nights a week, he allowed me to sit on the front porch, under the exceptionally bright light he had installed—almost a spotlight—for an hour, and only with boys who met with his approval. Gilbert was the first boy who spent time with me on the porch. My parents had made it very clear that there would be no handholding or kissing. Early on we did share a kiss and were busted by my mom, so after that we only sneaked small pecks. When he was sure my parents weren't looking, Gilbert would grab my hand and caress it and gently leave little kisses on my forehead. This went on for nine months.

Finally, one evening when we were sitting together on the porch, Gilbert told me that he had to go to California for a few weeks to help his mother. Before he left that night, we shared our first really passionate kiss on the lips. I felt butterflies. This kiss was a big deal in my life—and, as far as I was concerned, a real benchmark. I had a boyfriend who liked me; his picture was on my bedside table. It was exciting to wake up thinking about him, and I was so happy about it.

Then Gilbert was gone much longer than expected, and he didn't have the money to visit me. At first we talked on the phone somewhat regularly, but then after a while I didn't hear from him. He had promised to call when he was back, but he didn't. I was genuinely confused, not to mention hurt, about what had happened to him, so I phoned one of his older female relatives. She told me, "Gilbert is getting married, and I don't think he had the nerve to tell you." Hearing this, I was heartsick and devastated. I cried so hard that I think she was embarrassed.

I still remember running to my mother. "Mom, he is getting married!" I sobbed. On the day of the wedding, I sat inside my room feeling completely miserable and sorry for myself. From that day forward, memories of that first failed relationship made me question everything that had to do with love. Why did Gilbert need to find another girl? What was wrong with me? Why didn't he stay faithful to me? Why didn't he tell me the damn honest truth instead of just ghosting me? It was going to hurt no matter how he did it, but if he had told me the truth, my reactions might have been different. Gilbert was my first love, and I tried to do everything right. Well, that formula didn't work. But why didn't he return as he promised he would? Why, why, why? My anger, combined with all my questions surrounding Gilbert, drove me crazy. It would be years before I had any answers.

The next boy who paid attention to me was Marcos. During the summer before my senior year, I remember returning home from the radio station, driving my pride and joy—my very own white Pontiac convertible with white leather interior. Marcos, who lived close to me, was driving a large and very shiny black truck and going in the opposite direction. Loud Mexican music was blaring from his radio. In fact, loud Mexican music was always blaring from his radio. When he saw me, like a scene from a romantic movie, he did a quick and memorable U-turn, raced to catch up with me, and gestured for me to pull over. Before he got out of the truck to walk over to me, he revved his engine. Vahroom! Vahroom! Marcos, who was a real, as well as handsome, Mexican cowboy, loved to rev his engine. It always got my attention, as well as my mother's disapproval.

When Marcos asked for my number, I gave it to him. He called within twenty-four hours, and then he started calling every night at 5:30. We regularly talked for an hour or longer. Marcos thought it was very cool that I worked for one of his favorite radio stations. Before long, he started knocking on the door so we could sit together on that well-lit porch. Our little porch meetings went on for a very short period of time. And then Marcos went missing. Somebody said they thought he was in another state. But he didn't even say goodbye, let alone tell me where he was going.

Gilbert and Marcos—that was my entire dating experience. As an eighteen-year-old high school senior, I think I was probably the most innocent—totally clueless, actually—girl in Las Vegas.

My approach to the romantic world was pretty much totally based on what I had learned from telenovelas and romance novels. Even though on some level I knew it was unrealistic, at least a part of me believed that my prince was around the corner. And when we met, he would immediately recognize our "meant to be" connection and the rest of my life would unfold perfectly. This over-romanticized view of the world would ultimately pull me down some unfortunate paths.

And then I met Gianni, and everything got a lot more com-plicated.

At eighteen, thanks to my own insecurities combined with my father's front-porch spotlight, I had almost zero experience navigating adult romantic relationships. I understood without it being said that discussing sex was not something my mother was comfortable with. My mother was old-school traditional and probably even shyer about talking about sex than I was. End result: I knew nothing. Nothing! When I started menstruating, I even felt embarrassed to tell my mother. I was aware that she'd most likely never had these conversations with her own mother.

Nobody had ever warned me about life or what it feels like to be overcome with passion. Nobody had ever sat me down and said, "Here's something you should know: Watch out! When a guy tells you he loves you, it doesn't necessarily mean forever and ever!" Certainly, nobody had ever told me about hormones or what happens to your body, not to mention your brain, when you are totally turned on by an attractive male who is telling you he loves you while he's kissing your neck. I needed some serious advice, and I wasn't getting it.

I wanted to find love, but my expectations were unrealistic. The telenovela—or Hollywood—version of romance made me believe that Boy and Girl meet, fall in love, buy a house, raise babies, and live happily ever after. I didn't expect the complications, unhappiness, and general chaos that took over my life. What did Gianni expect? I have no idea, and, although I probably should have asked him, I didn't.

Gianni and me: Let's start with the simple facts, which by themselves were probably not all that simple.

Gianni was more than twenty years older than me—about the same age as my father, but that didn't matter to me. As far as I was concerned, he was amazing—smart, talented, and sophisticated. At the time I thought, I am so lucky that this very special man has chosen me. Now, of course, I look back and wonder why on earth he was interested in an innocent adolescent—which, of course, is precisely what my parents wondered at the time.

Like mine, Gianni's family came from Mexico. Our shared Latino culture should have given us something in common, but it didn't, because even though Gianni came from Mexico, he had a negative attitude toward anything Hispanic. For example, his real name was actually Miguel, but he legally changed it to Gianni and preferred to have people think he was Italian. It seemed a little weird to me, but hey, I was eighteen—what did I know about life and the choices people make? At the time, I was sure he had his reasons even if I didn't understand them. Later, of course, I did ask myself why someone who felt so strongly about not being identified as Latino would deliberately get involved with such a traditional Mexican girl. But I was so young and so happy to have an attractive man pay attention to me that I questioned very little about him or his intentions.

Gianni was a very good singer and an excellent musician—he played the bass, drums, piano, and sax, all at an expert level. He also wrote advertising jingles. I actually met him in my father's office when he came in to pitch the possibility of writing a jingle for my father's company. I didn't pay much attention to him at first; he was older, and it didn't even occur to me that he would be interested in me.

But then I started seeing him around the radio station, and I couldn't help but notice that he would always smile and stop to stay a few words to me. I sort of wondered, who is this guy? But I didn't think much about it. Then he told me that was doing commercials for some local businesses, and he asked me, "Could you work with me tonight doing voice-overs?"

Of course I said yes.

That night, we were in a recording studio at the station, and while we were working, he was very attentive. Having a grown man flirt with me was another first. I was so clueless about how men behave that I wasn't entirely sure that he was flirting. Was he really paying special attention to me, or was I imagining it? I remember that he tried to grab my hand, and I didn't know how to react or what to do. My stomach fluttered. God, I was so excited, I didn't want that evening to end.

Before I finally left to go home, he asked me a question, and I can still hear his tone of voice: "Would you go out to dinner with me?"

I responded with my own question. "Are you asking me on a date?"

"I am," he replied.

I became so nervous that I started stuttering. Then I froze up. I'd never been asked on a date before, and I didn't know what to say.

"Did you have fun with me?" He smiled at me.

"Yes," I answered him.

"Would you like to go out to dinner?" he asked me again

"Yes."

I lied to my parents. I told them I was working and met Gianni at the studio. He had a bright red sports car, and when he opened the car door for me, I remember thinking, well, this is nice! We went to an Italian restaurant. I was starving, but I was so shy about eating in front of him that I pecked at my food and ate almost nothing. I was a wreck, and dinner provided one awkward moment after another. I spilled a drink; I almost fell; I was so nervous that I could barely speak. I think about this now and wonder how I could not have read the signs. I started by lying to my parents. Lies are red flags. They are the start of all kinds of negative patterns. Clearly this relationship wasn't a good idea. But I had major lessons ahead, and boy, did I learn my lessons *so hard.*

When we went back to the studio together, Gianni looked into my eyes and said, "You are beautiful, innocent, and very sweet—I love that about you."

As we were about to part, each in our own car, he gave me a kiss on my forehead, which precipitated an attack of panicked laughter. I couldn't stop. This was all so new to me.

It was one of the last weeks of my senior year, and I left the last class of the day, as I always did, walking quickly, not looking to the left or the right and heading straight for my convertible. Sitting on my white leather front seat was an adorable little teddy bear with a festive red bow around his neck, along with a little red heart that said, "I love you." Next to the bear was a large bouquet of red roses and a note that read, "I'm falling in love with you." The note was unsigned, but of course I knew that there was only one person who could have written it. I had seen other girls get presents from guys—but nothing like this had ever happened to me.

Let me make it clear that Gianni's pursuit was over the top: He said everything I had ever dreamed of a boyfriend saying. How could I not think he was wonderful? And he sounded so passionate and sincere that I believed every word he uttered. We began spending more and more time together—mostly in the recording studio at the radio station. And then he romantically kissed me for the first time. I was so unsure of what to do that I clenched my teeth, and there was one awkward moment when our front teeth actually bumped into one another—thwack! I somehow quickly managed to figure out the whole kissing thing and responded to our first embrace by falling madly in love as only an insecure girl with low self-esteem can fall. I was sure that we were soul mates. What else could explain my feeling as though our hearts were attached? I continued to mislead my parents when I was with him, but from his many phone calls, they were beginning to figure out that something was going on, and they weren't happy about it. My mother actually thought he was sweet, but she also thought he was way too old for me, and not somebody who would be a good life partner for her daughter.

As soon as I graduated from high school, I began working full-time in the office of my parents' business; my plan was to begin attending a community college in the fall. In the meantime, Gianni was working all the time at dozens of different jobs.

Most of the time, Gianni played piano at various bars and venues, and he would invite me to come with him to watch. This was the Las Vegas nightlife that, until then, I had only heard about. It was an introduction to a world that seemed so glamorous and exciting. I was also in total awe of Gianni's talent and his ability to switch from instrument to instrument. After his shows, we would drive out to a higher elevation, where we could get an overview of the lights and the city; there we would sit in his car and neck and talk for hours. It was very romantic. He told me all his stories about life as a musician and how he wanted and planned to get ahead. "I'm going to fake it till I make it," he would say. I thought he was fascinating. He started teaching me how to play the drums, and when he stood behind me to show me how to hold the sticks, I got a sense of being with a man who was in control. One of the reasons I fell in love with him is because I believed he had so much to teach me. He even tried to turn me into a singer, but I was way too shy.

My All-or-Nothing Choice

Gianni and I had been involved for about three months when he phoned after my parents' strict "turn-off" hour of 8:00 P.M. My mother told me to get off the phone. My father said, "Calling at nine thirty is disrespectful. He needs to have more respect for this family." I was so flustered and embarrassed I didn't know what to do. Gianni asked me to please find a way to get out and meet him at the Walgreens near my house. I hung up the phone, waited about ten minutes, and convinced my mother that I absolutely needed something at the drugstore—implying that I was out of feminine hygiene products. He was waiting in an aisle of the drugstore—somewhere between cold remedies and baby aspirin. My heart was pounding.

"I can't do this anymore," he said. "I want to be with you. This situation is more than I can handle. Either come with me now, or I am going to leave here and go back to California or even Mexico." He looked deep into my eyes and repeated himself: "If you love me, you'll trust me and just come with me. If not, I'm leaving for Mexico and will never see you again." He absolutely sounded as though he meant every word he said.

It was my all-or-nothing choice. Did I lose him or lose my family? Did I hurt my parents by going off with Gianni? Or did I risk losing him forever? Just the idea of being without him made my stomach clench and filled me with pain and grief. But in retrospect, I realize that more than anything, what I really wanted in that moment was a sense of freedom and a different life. My parents were so strict, and I didn't have the courage to leave home by myself. Underneath the surface drama, Gianni gave me the opportunity I needed.

His plan involved the two of us going to Salt Lake City, where he said we would be able to stay with friends. I told myself that it would be like eloping and going on a honeymoon. We got into my car, stopped at the nearest gas station to fill the tank, and took off. "I don't care about anything but you," he said. As we drove, he serenaded me. If I had any hesitation, hearing his wonderful voice singing songs of love allowed me to push my doubts aside. With the top down, breathing in the cool night air, I also felt a new and wonderful sense of freedom. It lifted me up, and for those few hours at least I felt empowered and as though I was in charge of my own destiny.

In Salt Lake City, we did all the usual tourist things, exploring the city's landmarks and parks. Gianni's friends, who let us stay in their house, were kind and accepting of me. We also went to bed together, which I have to admit I didn't think was anywhere near as much fun as the hours we had spent necking in a car. It simply wasn't everything I expected. The earth absolutely did not move, and I couldn't hear waves crashing against the shore. I also couldn't shake my underlying concern that we were doing something that went against everything I was taught about sex being reserved to the sanctity of marriage, and my guilt and confusion may have been a factor in how I was feeling. I should add that sex wasn't the only thing making me feel guilty. During my time in Salt Lake City, I felt guilty about everything, particularly my poor parents, who I knew must have been worried sick. To this day, I still can't believe that I did that to them. They had no idea why I didn't return from the drugstore or where I was. I discovered later they were so upset that they called the police. I was also concerned about my sisters, particularly Lily, who always did everything with me. Recently she told me that my disappearance represented a major trauma in her life.

It was a week before Gianni and I finally returned to Vegas. I didn't know what to expect from my mom, but when I finally saw her, all she did was hug me tight and say, "Why would you do this to me, your father, your sisters, your brother? Why? You are worth so much more. He's not the one for you."

"Mom," I told her, "I love him. I really love him. I am sure he's the man I want to be with for life."

She was determined to make herself clear. "You don't know what love is. Go to college. There are other things you can do. You will meet other men—he is too old for you. You can study flamenco in Spain. We will help you do that." More than anything I had wanted to pursue flamenco, but even that offer from my mother failed to alter the hardheaded course I was on. I was rebellious. Deep down I knew I wasn't making the right decision, but I ignored that inner voice. And when we fail to listen to that inner voice, there are always serious consequences. And why didn't I listen to my mom, who always wanted the best for me? Life has taught me that the universe is always warning us and giving us help in our decision-making. I've learned that our gut feelings represent angels who are trying to protect us. We need to listen.

In retrospect, it's also interesting that my super traditional and religious parents did not say anything like, "You've been with the man, so marriage needs to be your first priority." They were so positive that Gianni wasn't right for me. In truth, I was also conflicted about the idea of marriage. On the one hand, I was embarrassed that people might think Gianni and I were "living in sin," so I encouraged people to think that we were married. However, in truth, I wasn't all that eager to get married. I was probably rebelling against the way in which I had been raised. As accustomed as I was to following all the traditional rules and regulations, I didn't want to live like that anymore, and in some ways, I began to be almost oppositional in my approach to the world. I wanted to feel free to make my own choices and decisions. But there was a huge problem: In the process of trying to find my freedom, I managed to lose even more of my sense of self. And my decision to run off with Gianni was making it more and more difficult to figure out who I was and what I truly wanted.

Losing Your Sense of Self

When I met Gianni, my sense of self was tenuous at best. I was so insecure, and after years of bullying, I had minimal self-esteem. With a head full of fantasies, fed by the books I read and movies I was watching in my spare time, I was deeply unprepared for what it meant to be in a relationship. As a young girl, I thought "being in love" meant that you had to give up all parts of yourself to make the other person happy. To keep Gianni happy, I was prepared to give up all my own interests and enthusiasms. I was prepared to lose my own sense of identity, not to mention my connection to others, including my family. He came first. I was a part of a family with strong values about what to do and how to live, but somehow Gianni's values became central to my life.

I didn't know how to say no to him, and I didn't really want to do so anyway. I gave up my own goals and my own dreams in order to do what I thought would make him happy. Without considering what I was actually doing, I gave away large pieces of myself because I thought that would strengthen our relationship—I actually thought that giving in was part of my role as a woman. I ended up feeling empty, angry, resentful, and unhappy. When you give up on your own dreams, you lose your inspiration, your creativity, your spark. You lose your *self.* It's like there's nobody home. Any relationship that requires you to give up or suppress those important parts of yourself is simply doomed to fail. In that situation, I wasn't my best self and didn't bring my best self to the relationship or anything else.

How I behaved with Gianni taught me that important lesson: Never give up your sense of self. Maintain your own interests, and stay true to your values and your core beliefs. Hang on to them as though your life depended on them—because it does. And know that the right relationship will bring out the best in both people—not limit each other. A healthy relationship provides a strong foundation to explore not only the world but who you are. Don't ever give up your sense of independences and your right to decide for yourself. Don't give up your opinions, your dreams and goals, or your relationships with family and friends. Lesson I learned: If your relationship is making you feel as though you are sacrificing any of those, that is a big warning sign that you are not making good choices for yourself.

Living Together

Finding a place in Vegas to live was one of the first issues Gianni and I faced. We managed to get an inexpensive short-term rental, but my father's advice about never throwing money away on rent rang in my ears, and almost immediately I began searching for a house to buy. The first few weeks together were good. In so many ways, Gianni continued to function as my teacher and guide. I loved the poetic side of his personality and his way with words. He also loved film and would rent movies. I will always remember watching those old black-and-white movies together—*Casablanca, Sabrina, Roman Holiday, It Happened One Night*. It introduced me to a whole other world.

Gianni was working a great deal at the hotels and other places on the strip, and I would go with him. It was fun. That was the good part. But there were other parts. It turned out that Gianni was extremely controlling. He had very definite ideas about how I should dress and look, commenting on everything I wore, often going so far as to pick out my outfits. "Wear this," he would say, handing me a dress before selecting exactly which shoes and earrings would go best with it. Gianni himself was meticulous about his grooming. (He put mousse on his eyelashes!) He also went shopping with me for clothes and had a lot to say about what I bought and how it should be worn. At first I was flattered and took his attention as a sign of his love. Then, I began to feel he was treating me like I was a doll he owned. We went out almost every night, and he always wanted me to be fully made up, wearing jewelry, and dressed to the nines. "We look good together," he would say.

One of the few things we didn't do together was go house hunting. Gianni thought buying a house was a crazy idea, but he did nothing to stop my searching. This was a time in Vegas, before the housing crash, when the primary requirement for getting a mortgage was that you were breathing. Even though I was only eighteen, I had money in the bank and a steady salary from my father's business. Because Gianni didn't have a regular job, adding his name to the mortgage would have only complicated matters. In an amazingly short time, I found a three-bedroom, two-bath house in a brand-new development. Although Gianni wasn't enthusiastic, he didn't say, "Don't do it," either. He also didn't say, "Let's do this together." Later, I would be happy that my name was the only one on the deed, but at the time it really didn't seem like a big deal, and I thought it would all get ironed out in the future. One of the best things about the house was that one of the bedrooms could be turned into Gianni's full-time music studio—a place where he could work without having to pay someone else additional rent.

During our first weeks together, I felt as though Gianni loved me and, for perhaps the first time in my life, began to be a little more comfortable in my own body. Not so comfortable, however, that I was ever able to get dressed or undressed in front of him. Gianni would cheerfully walk around buck naked—I, on the other hand, was always covered up. There is one other thing I should mention: In the early days of our relationship, when we went everywhere together, Gianni was jealous. One day, we had an appointment with a real estate agent who wanted to create a commercial using one of Gianni's jingles. We all met at a coffee shop, but the agent then decided we needed to see one of his properties. He had no clue that Gianni and I were a couple, and when we stood up to leave in order to drive to the property, he gestured to me to get in his car. "Don't worry," he said to Gianni as he guided me to his car. "I've got her. Just follow me."

What was I thinking? Not much. After all, it was only a ten-minute car ride. I was trying to be very nice to the guy because I was trying to help Gianni make the sale. It honestly didn't occur to me that the agent might be coming on to me. But even if it had, I wasn't flirting with him. After we finally said goodbye, Gianni was furious. His voice was harsh, and he said, "Don't you ever do anything like that to me again." That was probably the first time I saw that side of his personality. He acted like I had cheated on him. His anger was so real that he actually made me feel as if I had done just that. He stormed out of the house, slamming the door as he left. I sincerely worried that he was going to leave me and sat home for the entire day waiting for the phone to ring. Oh my God, I thought, this relationship is ruined and it's all my fault. As each hour passed, I became more and more anxious. Where was he? What was he doing? Was he going to return? Paralyzing anxiety and worry about Gianni's whereabouts would turn out to be one of the primary ongoing features of our relationship, but this was the first time I sat there waiting, hugging the phone and hoping it would ring.

I quickly adapted my behavior to take his jealousy into consideration. It didn't take me long to figure out that I shouldn't interact with any other men, so I was very careful about that. But it wasn't just men who made Gianni jealous. He basically didn't want me to relate to anyone but him. He would get annoyed and angry if I wanted to visit my family, so my relationship with my parents became more strained and distant. He didn't want to spend time with them or have them involved in our life in any way, and I tried to accommodate his wishes.

Along with this, Gianni was totally obsessed with getting me pregnant. I was so young and we had been together such a short time that I wasn't sure that I was ready for a pregnancy. But I wanted to please him.

"Well, do you think you are pregnant?" he would ask at regular intervals.

"No," I would tell him sadly.

"Why isn't it happening?" he would ask.

These exchanges made me feel like I was failing him and the relationship. At the time I didn't question his urgent need to get me pregnant and actually took it for granted that it was part of his male prerogative and an attempt on his part to "cement" our loving connection. It took us about four months, and when it happened, I didn't need a pregnancy test or a trip to the doctor to confirm anything because I was almost immediately struck by a brutal case of morning sickness. It was really not accurate to call it morning sickness because hours of nausea and waves of vomiting happened all day and all night. And then I started to gain weight—and more weight, which was amazing since it seemed to me that I was eating next to nothing. But much of the food that was staying down was in the category of high-calorie carbohydrates—comfort food that I was mostly eating late at night, when I felt a little bit less nauseous.

I think about my time with Gianni as being a major life lesson. Here's some of what I learned.

Don't expect your life to come together like a romantic movie. Just because a guy says all the things you want to hear doesn't mean he's sincere or that he's the right person for you.

When you meet someone you like, take your time before you give your heart away. If a relationship is meant to happen, it will happen.

Don't let loneliness direct your life. As a young girl, I felt so deprived and wanted a boyfriend so badly, I would probably have responded to anyone who said, "I want to be with you." This is always a mistake.

Listen to your inner voice and pay attention to your intuition. I knew that something was off when Gianni started pursuing me. Why was he pushing so hard to move the relationship to the next level? We had known each other such a short time—why was he being so reckless? When he asked me to run off with him, I absolutely knew it wasn't what I should be doing. I felt left out, watching everyone else date, and let fear be the decision-maker in my life when I should have stepped back and said, "Not so fast!"

Don't give up your dreams just because someone is trying to tie you down. Why was I so willing to let go of the things I wanted so much to do—like go to school and study flamenco? It's always important to follow your dreams. Get to know *you*—what do you like? What do you want?

Don't be so afraid of losing someone that you go along with whatever the other person wants. It's healthy to say, "No, thank you," when something (or someone) on offer is really not of interest to you.

Don't be afraid of saying that you are not ready to move forward. If you are not ready, you are not ready. Anyone who really loves and respects you will understand. They will respect you and wait.

At the slightest sign that you are involved with a controlling person, get professional help about what you should do to protect yourself. Don't ever confuse control with love. Sometimes we confuse control with love out of our own loneliness.

Take your time; don't rush. Allow time to get to know the people you meet. Find out more about their values, and watch what they do, not just what they say.

Your First Chance Isn't Your Last Chance

When an exciting opportunity crosses our path and we think we want it, we sometimes reach out too quickly to grab at it, scared that if we don't do so, we'll never get another chance. But in life, there are always other chances—and often better ones. A woman who is sure of herself realizes that taking her time and being sure of what she wants and where she is going is the wiser move.

Your first chance is not your last chance! In fact, our first anything should be treated as just that—our first try and a great learning experience. Grabbing at the first thing that crosses your path, whether it's love, a job, or a last-minute date for Saturday night, without thinking it through isn't showing yourself the respect you deserve. Stay courageous and don't be afraid to say no. Too many times in life, when we grab at those first chances, we are settling—and on some level, we know we are settling. That's how we end up in unhappy situations, wishing we had waited for those better opportunities that will be coming along. Set yourself up for success. And recognize when you are making a fear-based decision. Ask yourself, *Am I coming from a place of inspiration or desperation?*

Tell yourself: *I am worthy of healthy love and respect.*

And make yourself a promise today: *I will never settle for less than I deserve.*

CHAPTER 6

Rejection Is Just a Redirection

THE PREGNANCY ALMOST IMMEDIATELY CHANGED EVERYthing in our relationship. My nausea and fatigue made it almost impossible for me to go with Gianni to his nightly gigs, so we rarely did anything as a couple. He came home in the early-morning hours and slept late, which meant we weren't even in the house at the same time that often. I continued to work for my parents, where I had easy access to a bathroom, but the bouts of nausea made it difficult for me to go much of anyplace else. At first Gianni was very sweet about the baby. He would ask me to sit next to him while he played the piano, singing to my belly and telling me that it was good for a baby to get that kind of early exposure to music. But at the same time, I couldn't help but notice that emotionally he was different with me—less caring and more fault finding . . . much more fault finding. This was such a shock that I didn't know what to think or how to act. My initial reaction was to try to please him, something that was becoming more and more difficult to do.

My big question: Why wasn't the man who was so determined to get me pregnant overjoyed now that I was? Because he wasn't. In fact, almost from the first instant the pregnancy was confirmed, Gianni started a noticeable withdrawal. I didn't understand what was happening or why. I also didn't have anybody to talk to about our problems and what I was feeling. My parents had been so opposed to the relationship that I didn't want to confide in them or worry them. I still hoped that their relationship with Gianni would improve over time and didn't want to do anything to jeopardize that possibility. I continued to be friendly with Genesis and talked to her some, but our lives were now so different that we had turned into phone friends, and I didn't feel comfortable burdening her.

Gianni was with me the day I got my first ultrasound. He sat there and looked at the little screen. "See," the doctor said, "you can see the beating heart. Do you want to know the sex?"

"Yes," I quickly replied. I was genuinely excited.

"It's a girl," he told me.

I looked over at Gianni, hoping against hope that our eyes would meet with joy. But that's not what happened. Gianni stared at the little being whose heartbeat was blipping on the screen. The look on his face was one of pure horror. It sent a cold chill through my body. On a deep, very primal level, I somehow knew that this was the end of our relationship, but I didn't want to face it.

As the pregnancy progressed, I went almost nowhere with Gianni, but he still went out just about every night. Even worse, he began drinking, and very heavily. My evenings were spent sitting in our house, which I was trying to decorate for our family, fighting the nausea and waiting for Gianni to get home, all the while feeling utterly alone and rejected. Usually I would fall asleep, frequently on the couch. He would finally walk through the door after 4:00 A.M., completely wasted more often than not. There were too many times when friends would carry him home, dead drunk, and drop him on the floor.

I was assaulted by a wide range of negative emotions—fear, loneliness, depression, and anger, as well as uncertainty about how I could fix the situation. I didn't know what had happened to the man who had said, "I don't care about anything but you." How could I get him back? Occasionally, along about midnight, I would go out searching the streets of Las Vegas, cruising past bars and nightclubs where I believed he might be playing. I was also concerned that he might be having an affair, and I wanted to know the truth about what he was doing. Once I saw him with a man, his hand on the man's back. Another time, Genesis came with me, and we went to the venue where he was playing. He was standing outside with a woman. He was laughing and clearly having a wonderful time. Genesis said to me, "This is toxic. You need to get out of this relationship."

Sometimes it feels as though my primary memory of the relationship is that Gianni was out getting hammered, and I was driving around trying to find him. One night, at 2:00 A.M., sobbing, I got into my car and went out looking for him. I was speeding down Las Vegas Boulevard when a cop pulled me over. The officer took one look at my tears and my obviously pregnant body and he said, "What are you doing? You're pregnant. You could kill your baby driving this way!" I just started sobbing louder and told him that I was looking for Gianni, who never came home anymore.

The cop insisted that I drive back home. He went so far as to follow me to make sure I got there. He walked me to the door. "Just screw this guy for doing this sh*t to you while you are pregnant," he said. "Forget him. You and your baby deserve better." It was probably good advice, but not so easy to follow.

What Did I Really Know About the Man?

At home, I would do those things that millions of other pained, scared, and jealous women have done: I turned into a detective. I went through his coat pockets, I went through his wallet, I went through every piece of paper on which he might have scribbled any numbers. I was worried that he was seeing someone else, and I did everything I could to figure out if that was the case. We had set up the third bedroom as his private music studio, so I went through everything there. That's when I found the stack of magazines—male porn hidden in the back of a closet! Was it possible that something else was going on?

In January, when the new semester started, I moved forward with my plan to take classes at the community college. But it was impossible. For one thing, my morning sickness continued; for another, I had already gained so much weight that I could no longer fit into the student chairs that were assigned. They were simply too tiny for my growing body. The first time I went to a class, it was obvious the chair wasn't going to work. Somebody carried in a small table with a separate chair and put it in front of the room, where my hugeness was on display for everyone to see. It was total humiliation.

And yes, there were still moments when Gianni and I talked and were affectionate with each other, and those moments gave me hope that everything would smooth out and we would end up as a happily married couple. But most of the time, Gianni and I were like ships passing in the night. He left the house to go to work around seven at night, returning well after 4:00 A.M. He would sleep until close to noon, when he would grab something to eat and go to the gym, returning in the afternoon for a few hours before leaving again.

My schedule was very different. I had to be at my parents' office by 9:00 A.M. Sometimes I would return home so we could have lunch together. Gianni, who continued to exercise regularly and always worried about his health, would be eating salad while I would be chewing on something in the carbohydrate family, which Gianni would criticize. We had also started arguing about lots of small stuff. Gianni would complain about everything going wrong in his life and find a way to hold me responsible. Consequently, I walked on eggshells. From his point of view, I'd created a long list of problems for him. He had gained weight—my fault; clients had complained about his work—my fault; he didn't have time to do everything he wanted to do—my fault; and yes, he was drinking too much—again it was my fault. And why, he wanted to know, was I prying and asking him so many questions? In the meantime, I was beginning to ask myself the all-important question: Was he finding fault because he was looking for an excuse to get out?

For the most part, I didn't confront Gianni in any way. I didn't want to make trouble, because more than anything, I was afraid of losing him. However, all these thoughts kept going through my head, and one day I came into his studio while he was playing the piano. I just walked up to him and told him that I had found all those magazines. I asked him if he was involved with someone else. I asked him if he was gay and whether he was seeing anyone specifically. He stopped playing. "Just tell me, yes or no," I pleaded. "What's going on?" He started crying and couldn't look me in the eye. He just nodded. I never really understood what his tears or his nod meant. Was he telling me that he was gay? Was he telling me that he was in a relationship with a specific person? Was that person male or female? I could never completely understand his reactions. I also had to ask myself the other question that loomed in my brain: Was he just so turned off by my very overweight and pregnant body that he wanted nothing more to do with me?

Soon after that—just a few days after my twentieth birthday—Gianni told me he had to go to Mexico for a job. I was eight months pregnant—unbelievably anxious and scared and terrified about just about everything.

"I'll be back in a week," he said.

"But the baby could be born any day," I said, telling him something he already knew.

"This could be very important to my career," he replied, "and I can't afford not to go."

He booked a round-trip ticket, and I drove him to the airport. His goodbye hug felt impersonal and cold.

"I'll call you," he said.

Well, he didn't call. And he didn't return. I tried calling the airline to see if he had taken the booked return flight, but they wouldn't tell me anything. When I called his phone, there was no answer, but the ring was a little different, which made me believe he was still in Mexico. I tried phoning every single possible person who might know where he was. They all said that they didn't know. If anything that made me realize even more how little I knew about Gianni. I didn't, for example, know one single person in his family, and he had rarely talked about them. There was nobody in his family I could call.

Becoming a Mother

Already beside myself with fear and super-high anxiety, I went into labor.

I phoned my parents and asked them to meet me at the hospital. For reasons I can't even begin to explain, I was still hoping that everything would work out with Gianni, so I was still lying to them.

"Gianni is in Mexico," I told them. "We didn't expect anything to happen this quickly. And I can't reach him." My sad little fantasy was that Gianni would miraculously show up as Super Dad and a completely committed family man, and I didn't want my mother and father to be angrier with him than they were already.

I don't want to sound overly dramatic, but I was in the hospital in labor for a day, but it felt like a week. I wanted to tough it out without anything to kill the pain, but toward the end, I was screaming for an epidural, which helped with the labor pains, but it did nothing for the emotional grief that was ripping through my body. The most painful part of my hospital stay was watching all the happy couples holding hands. Why was I alone? What had I done to create this situation?

By the time my baby was born, I was crying so hard I couldn't even name her, so I told my mother to do it. "Isabella," she said.

"Isabella. Bella for short," I repeated. I was happy that it was such a beautiful name.

When it came time to go home and my parents asked about Gianni's whereabouts, I complained about the terrible phone service to Mexico, saying I couldn't reach him.

An aide arrived with a wheelchair so my father could wheel my beautiful Bella and me out of the hospital. And I didn't fit. They had to go find an even bigger chair. But that wasn't the worst part. The worst part was watching all those smiling husbands pushing their beaming wives and new babies. In the meantime, I was in a super-size wheelchair—terrified, trying not to cry, and being pushed by my exceptionally patient father.

My father drove me home, tried to help me as much as possible, and then he left. I was all alone in a quiet and lonely house. All I could hear was my unending inner dialogue. What happened? Why did Gianni change? Why did he appear to be one type of person and then turn into another? Was it all my fault? What were the reasons? Was my weight responsible? Was he in a relationship with somebody else? Did he really prefer men? Did he run because I became pregnant and the relationship became too real for him to handle? All I had wanted was a marriage like my parents'. WHAT HAPPENED?! Was he just profoundly full of sh*t from day one?

It had only been a little more than a year since that afternoon that I skipped happily out of my Senior Civics class and found the roses and the bear on the seat of my car. The bear, the note, and one dried rose were all in a memory box I kept in my closet. The box held the mementos from our relationship. I pulled it all out of the closet and destroyed it, burning it in a fire in the backyard. The bear was too big to burn, so I cut it into tiny pieces. I was furious and screaming. Somehow, Bella slept through my outrage, which ended with a sea of sobs.

About a week later, I went into my parents' office to visit. I was still lying to my parents about Gianni's whereabouts, but a woman came in briefly to congratulate me on the baby. "You and your husband must be so happy," she said. I nodded and smiled. As I did so, the lie I was telling was tearing into me. It felt like a knife stuck into my stomach. Since Bella's birth, each time someone referred to my "husband," the knife twisted a little deeper.

After the woman left, I went into the bathroom, looked at myself in the mirror, and started crying louder and louder. It was a complete and total emotional breakdown featuring loud sobbing, wall hitting, and more than a few screams of "Why? Why? Why?" I was so pained and so angry. And I finally had to admit the truth to my family—the family I had so deeply hurt by running off with Gianni. They must have suspected something was wrong, but they had said nothing. My mother came into the bathroom, and as I stood there crying, she put her arms around me and cried along with me.

After I finally stopped crying and went back home, I methodically started getting rid of Gianni's stuff. I called Gianni's business partner, who came and took all his musical instruments. Then I phoned my good friend Manuel, a strong, dependable buddy who worked for my parents. He came and took charge of all the clothing and personal items. He cleaned out the closet. I knew that Manuel would either use all the items or find others who could.

Gianni did return. Once. When Bella was a few months old, she was baptized, and we had a small christening party for her. I have no idea how or why Gianni came back. I didn't even know if it was a total coincidence that he returned when we were having a party or if someone had told him about it. There were at least thirty people there, some of whom had not yet been told that Gianni and I had split. I was so shocked to see him that I didn't know what to say. I also didn't want to embarrass my parents by making a scene. In my head, I was hoping and expecting that there would be a moment when we would be able to talk. But he left so quickly that it wasn't possible. It was a "now you see him, now you don't" experience. Someplace there is one photo of him holding Bella. I don't think he stayed long enough to have a piece of cake.

And that was it. Gianni was gone.

But the Depression Remained

Many relationships end without any true resolution, but how many end without even a single conversation? I couldn't reach Gianni. I had so much I wanted to say, but I couldn't talk to him; I couldn't tell him how he had made me feel; I couldn't ask him anything. I felt as though my heart was screaming. I was without answers or any true understanding. This was one of the darkest periods of my life. Most nights, once I put Bella to bed, my unhappiness took over. To this day, the same questions about Gianni and our relationship remain unanswered.

Back then I spent many more hours than I should have going over and over the details of our relationship and what had happened. I was ruminating incessantly, my brain filled with dozens of what-ifs. What could I have done differently? What should I have done differently? How could I have changed the outcome? What would have happened if I confronted him the first time he came home late? What would have happened if I stopped him at Bella's christening party and didn't let him leave?

I couldn't come to terms with the fact that poetic and sensitive Gianni, who insisted on getting me pregnant, had ended up walking away as though our relationship was a one-night stand. What had he been doing with me? What the f*ck had he been thinking? And, of course, what the f*ck had I been thinking to go off with him the way I had? Anger and sadness would all get mixed together in a sleep-defying combination. I remember many bouts of truly ugly crying that lasted until I finally sobbed myself to sleep.

I was so overwhelmed with loneliness that I always kept the television on and slept with Univision providing background sound and company. My misery was so complete that I became convinced I was dying and kept thinking, What is going to happen to Bella? In my early twenties, I signed up for a large insurance policy. As young as I was, my weight meant that I couldn't get a good insurance policy without having a bunch of medical tests. I was relieved when the policy was finally issued. If I died, at least my daughter would have some money for her future.

My bedroom became my spiritual retreat, and at night I would burn incense as well as blessed candles. I liked feeling as though I had angels on my side and was receiving some divine support. No question about it—I needed all the help I could get.

I've talked to so very many women, and men, who have struggled to recover from romantic breakups that left them reeling. I wish there was a way to wave a magic wand and make all that pain disappear.

What I Learned the Hard Way About Healing a Broken Heart

You can't make another person stay with you—no matter how much you want them to stay. And trust me, there will come a day when you will be grateful that the relationship ended and you are not stuck with the wrong person.

If someone doesn't give you an explanation, it doesn't mean that you are not worth an explanation. It means that the one you loved was a total d**khead at that moment of their life.

Healing doesn't happen overnight.

Recognize that you are grieving your romanticized version of what you thought the relationship was—this has little or nothing to do with reality.

Some people and memories are best left in the past.

If you keep focusing on your fantasized version of the relationship, you are inviting more hurt into your life.

Being by yourself is much better than being with the wrong person.

Understand that some days will be worse than others.

This painful ending is God's way of protecting you. It could have been much worse if you stayed together.

Big Lesson: Rejection is just a redirection.

Rejection Is Just a Redirection

You don't always get what you think you want. And so what?

Here's a major truth: If you were meant to be together, you would be together. When a relationship ends, you are being given a great opportunity to learn some major lessons from what happened. These lessons are personalized just for you, so pay attention, learn your lesson, and it's guaranteed that your life will change for the better. This is your time to make a firm commitment to heal and find happiness in your future.

Start redirecting your life by reconnecting with supportive people who truly love you and spend more time with them. Think about all the things you want to do, from cleaning your closets, to getting a new hairstyle, to taking a vacation, signing up for new classes, or finding new hobbies. It's all about creating new experiences in your life—ones full of positivity and excitement. New doors are going to be opening for you.

Rejections happen to all of us in all areas and different levels. We don't always get the romantic partners or friends we think we want. The jobs we think we want are not always offered to us. Everyone gets fired, turned down, or let go.

It may not be immediately obvious, but everything that happens to us—including rejection—happens for a reason. It's always to make you a better human being, give you greater wisdom for handling your future, and help you get on a happier path—the one you really deserve.

CHAPTER 7

Don't Allow Fear to Become Your GPS

AFTER BELLA WAS BORN, THERE WAS ABSOLUTELY NO ROmance in my life for almost three years—no dates or anything else. My entire focus was on my daughter and making a living. Let's face it: I was scared. Actually, I was terrified. As much as I wanted a settled family life like my parents, I didn't believe it was ever going to happen for me, and I was afraid to take any more risks. But as afraid as I was of another failed relationship, I was probably even more scared of being alone for the rest of my life. I was so lonely. I didn't want to spend the rest of my life with Univision as my primary companion.

Anthony came into my life when Bella was about three. We started out as friends and eventually became best friends. I was happy that Anthony, who was ready and willing to assume a role in my life, was there. Anthony, who was blond, didn't look Latino and strangers were often startled when he started speaking fluent Spanish. He was a good, kind guy, and my whole family liked him; he even went to work for my father.

Anthony, who was also very caring to Bella, evolved into my dependable, loving boyfriend. I loved that he was always a gentleman. I loved that on Valentine's Day he sent me the biggest bouquet of roses I have ever seen. When Bella got sick and threw up all over my car, I loved that he helped clean it up and that he went out and bought her Pedialyte without my asking. I loved that he never did or said anything to make me feel bad about my weight. He was my boyfriend, and he was a good boyfriend.

There were so many good things about Anthony, ranging from his compassionate heart to his sense of humor. He was funny and fun to be with. I was a big Jim Carrey fan, and I will never forget the night that the two of us were on my bed watching *Dumb and Dumber*. We both laughed so hard we almost fell on the floor. I was very heavy when I met Anthony and very ashamed of the size of my hips, which were so large that sometimes strangers—usually mean guys—stopped and made rude comments. People even pulled out cameras to take pictures of me. It would make me wish that I could somehow disappear. Anthony would always defend me. One time he almost got into a fight with some stranger who made fun of my hips.

"Please ignore it," I begged him.

"I'm tired of ignoring it," he responded. Anthony turned to the guy. "You have to learn to respect women," he said.

"I don't have to respect no fat bitch," the guy responded.

By then Anthony was furious and, using both hands, gave the guy a push.

When the guy realized just how angry Anthony was, he backed off.

We were going out more than a year when my dad, who continued to be a huge advocate of the self-empowerment movement, gifted Anthony with a seminar. The night Anthony graduated from the seminar, I attended to show my support, along with his aunt Carina, who had also become one of my best friends. At the end of the evening, as is common at these seminars, participants were asked to stand and share something they had learned. When it was Anthony's turn, he stood and introduced me. "This is my girlfriend," he said. "This week taught me to be more open with my feelings and to appreciate the people in my life. I've become a better man because of Rosie and her family. They've given me so much and also showed me that it's important to be brave enough to take the next step." Then he got down on one knee and took out the ring he had already purchased. "Rosie," he said, "will you marry me?" People started screaming and applauding. Anthony was my best friend, and I said yes. How could I say anything else?

We had a large wedding in a beautiful garden. Almost everything was white—including lots of white flowers. I wore a white dress with my hair pinned up with flowers. Bella was wearing a tulle dress that was white and hot pink; her hair was also pinned up. My sisters, Priscilla and Lily, were my bridesmaids, and we were married by a nondenominational minister friend. There was even a DJ for dancing. The two families genuinely liked each other, and everybody was happy. I absolutely loved his aunt, who often came on Sundays to cook beautiful breakfasts for everybody.

At first, everything was good. Anthony had been told that he was sterile and would never be able to have children. Anthony believed his doctors, and I believed Anthony. Because I was happy and grateful that my new husband was so genuinely kind, I was okay with the thought that Bella would be my only natural child. We were married more than two years when I started to experience lower back pain and what I thought was an unusually heavy and painful menstrual period. I went to a new gynecologist, who examined me and said that he was almost certain I was having a miscarriage. I was positive that the doctor was mistaken because, after all, Anthony couldn't have kids. I didn't even tell Anthony because I didn't want to upset him, and the problem seemed to resolve itself. Then, a few weeks later, my back started bothering me again. It hurt so much, and I was so uncomfortable that I went to an emergency room hoping to get painkillers. They took blood to run some tests, asking me about my menstrual cycle and whether I thought I could be pregnant. "No way," I told them. "My husband is sterile." About an hour later, they came back to tell me that my hormone level indicated that I might be pregnant. I told Anthony what was going on, and when I was advised to have an ultrasound, Anthony was with me for the procedure. The technician started the ultrasound, and then boom, there on the screen was Valentino! I told them about the heavy bleeding a month or so earlier, and they explained that it is sometimes possible for a woman to become pregnant with twins—to miscarry one and continue to carry the other. I remember that Anthony started crying—sadness at the loss of one baby and joy that there was another little baby growing inside me. It was a quiet ride home as we both thought long and hard about the changes that were going to take place.

Becoming More of an Expert at Failed Relationships

It was a very different pregnancy from the one I experienced with Bella. I had very little morning sickness, but as the pregnancy progressed, I became more and more emotional—probably a combination of the hormones and my memories of everything that happened when I was pregnant with Bella. Then suddenly, out of the blue, I found myself very fearful of losing Anthony just as I had lost Gianni, and as I began to relive the past, I also began nagging Anthony about small stuff. For example, I complained about having to ask Anthony to help with the dishes—why wasn't he doing it on his own? I'm sorry to say that I turned into more and more of a nag. But Anthony was doing some changing on his own—becoming more distant and withdrawn. He was backing away while I simultaneously began to pack on those extra pregnancy pounds. In truth, I don't know what happened first: Was I nagging because Anthony was backing away, or was Anthony backing away because I was nagging? Whatever actually caused the problems between us, our relationship started to go south in much the same way that my relationship with Gianni had.

My first clue that we might have a major problem came when Anthony received a phone call that I found genuinely disturbing. We had just returned from my grandmother's funeral, so I was already upset. He picked up his phone. "Hello," he said. Then almost immediately he added, "You're going to have to call back when I'm in the office."

I could hear the voice of the person on the other end of the phone. It was very faint, but I could definitely hear a woman asking, "Is she there?"

"Yes," he replied before hanging up the phone.

I looked at him. For a moment, I didn't know what to think. The whole phone exchange took seconds; the voice on the phone was indistinct. I didn't trust what I heard; I thought Anthony was the last person in the world who would cheat. It had all happened so quickly that it didn't fully register. I was confused, but there was no question that it also made me fearful and put me on alert. I couldn't help thinking about everything that had been going on. Anthony, for example, had been leaving the house for work more than an hour earlier than he used to. I wondered what that was all about. My insecurity was fanned, which in turn made me pick quarrels and nag more. I hoped that Anthony and I could discuss our relationship and come to some understanding, but Anthony was silent and interpreted my efforts to "talk" as more nagging.

I was about six months pregnant when Anthony announced that it was all too much. "I can't handle it," he said. "I just need *space*." He left the house telling me that he wanted to spend some time alone.

Anthony's retreat put me in full anxiety and terror mode, and the very next day, I began to have contractions. The doctor who examined me said that it was too soon to give birth; he put me on bed rest and gave me some injections that might control the contractions, telling me that Valentino needed more safe growing time.

While all this was happening, I didn't have any idea about what Anthony might be doing or thinking. I was frightened about losing him and remember calling his aunt on a regular basis. She kept telling me to relax. "Many men," she said, "become nervous at the idea of becoming fathers. Just take it easy. Calm down, take a deep breath, and take care of yourself."

It was impossible for me to calm down. Once again, I felt totally alone, and it was all too reminiscent of my last pregnancy. I knew something was going on, but I didn't know what. I was afraid of another major surprise, and needed more information. An idea crossed my mind—Private Investigator. So that's what I did. I had no idea how to find a PI and with shaking hands turned to the old standby, the Yellow Pages, which still existed. I got lucky. The private investigator I called turned out to be as professional as he was kind. He told me that he would get back to me within seven to ten days.

A little more than a week later, the investigator called and we set up an appointment. He had serious information. Anthony *was* seeing someone—a woman who worked as a secretary in Vegas. He had photos of Anthony, including some of him with his aunt as well as the woman out partying. Seeing those photos of my husband, I literally felt my heart drop. It took my breath away. The fact that his aunt Carina, knew what was going on made it all the worse. In many ways, I think I was as much hurt by Carina, my friend and confidante, as I was by Anthony. I took her lying and betrayal very hard.

I couldn't control my crying—nor could I stop the very painful contractions that began within twenty-four hours. I called my father, who took me to the hospital while my mother stayed with Bella. My labor was quick, intense, and traumatic, ending with an emergency

C-section. Little Valentino weighed two-point-four pounds and would have to stay in the hospital until he weighed four pounds. Once again, my response to giving birth involved frequent bouts of sobbing. When people came to visit, I discovered that several of them already knew that Anthony was having an affair. They thought it was just a little bit of male "acting out" and hadn't wanted to hurt me by telling me. Learning about that made me cry even more.

Valentino was born in the early afternoon. Within hours, I was surrounded by supportive parents, family, and friends, and I was sobbing my heart out. Twice! How could this have happened to me twice?! Someone must have told Anthony that I had given birth, because he showed up in the early evening. When a close family friend saw Anthony standing at the door, he walked over and slammed the door in his face and wouldn't let him enter. That was it! The end of a marriage to someone I had considered my best friend!!! Anthony made a few feeble attempts to see Valentino, but he had emotionally moved on, and it was over. When Valentino was finally able to leave the hospital, I was overwhelmed with feelings of abandonment, loneliness, and fear. There I was, sitting in a wheelchair, carrying my baby. Tears were rolling down my face while I was once again being pushed by my father.

Of course I was extremely hurt and depressed about the end of my marriage to Anthony, but I have to acknowledge that I wasn't nearly as devastated and completely heartbroken as I had been with Gianni. I had been happy with Anthony and had truly loved him. If he hadn't cheated, I would still be married to him. But I had never been madly in love with Anthony. I couldn't help but wonder if that had played a part in the final outcome of our marriage. Maybe he needed to be with a woman who was overcome with butterflies whenever she looked at him. I worried that he may have deserved more than I gave him. I loved him, but I had never been crazy about him. He was a good man who did a stupid thing. I sincerely hope that he is happy.

I felt so many things after Anthony left me—shock, surprise, betrayal, and hurt. But more than anything else, I was afraid—terrified at the prospect of loneliness and living the rest of my life without a partner. My goals hadn't changed: More than anything else, I still wanted a family. Anthony, Bella, and I had been a family. When Anthony took off, I was incredibly lonely. It felt as though I had lost more than a husband; I lost my family. I wanted a husband, and my children needed a father. After Gianni, I didn't date anyone else for several years, but after Anthony, it was very different.

Rebound

Anthony was out of my life for only a few months when Marcos—who I remembered as the teenage boy who had always announced his arrival by revving the engine of his shiny black truck—reappeared. Some things change, because Marcos now drove a white truck. Marcos, who owned a home improvement business, had actually once briefly showed up at my door soliciting business when I was still married to Anthony.

"Who is he?" he asked of Anthony.

"My husband," I replied.

"I can't believe you married him," he told me. "I was going to marry you—why didn't you wait for me?"

"Huh?" My memory was that Marcos had vanished from my life without saying a word. On the day that Marcos appeared in front of the door of the house I shared with Anthony, I don't think we said much of anything else before Marcos once again turned and walked away, but it turns out that it was not forever.

After Anthony and I split up, Marcos and I accidentally ran into each other. Valentino was only a few months old when we started dating. Rebound relationship, no question about it. Now, if I were to be coaching a client who was jumping into a serious relationship so soon after another had ended, I would advise that person to slow down. But more than anything else I was afraid of being alone, and I was moving very fast. So once again, I allowed my fear of loneliness to direct my life.

But let's not discount the fact that there were many things about Marcos that I genuinely liked and admired. He was extraordinarily hardworking, competent, capable, and very manly. He had his own business and lived on a ranch he owned. He seemed to have his act together. And the fact that he had fabulous sparkly eyes and appeared very sure of himself certainly didn't detract from his appeal.

For our first date, Marcos invited me to his ranch outside of Vegas. I was pushing Valentino in a stroller while Bella was running around, overjoyed to be able to pat the horses. It was good to be out in the fresh air, appreciating nature. I looked at Marcos, and there were many positives. We were both from the same Mexican culture; he was very accepting of my children. In no way did he ever do or say anything that made me feel that they were less than welcome. As a preemie, Valentino was already showing signs of being challenged, and Marcos was supportive and helpful. It was also important to me that he had been interested in me since I was a teenager—that had to count for something. And let's not forget my weight. After Valentino's birth, I weighed about 360 pounds. I was so heavy that I was embarrassed and uncomfortable about ever being seen in public. I never wanted to go anywhere, and Marcos didn't seem to mind the social limitations of being romantically involved with me. Bottom line: Fearful of being alone, I desperately wanted a relationship and a real family, and Marcos was there, sending me roses and telling me he loved me.

Let's be honest here: There was another very specific reason that helps explain why I married Marcos. I got pregnant. To his credit, he immediately stepped up. When I told Marcos about the pregnancy, he said, "I can't believe this happened. But let's do this right. I'm not running away. Let's try to make this work." But I had no idea what I was about to step into.

We had a large wedding reception, which Marcos planned. He invited most of his family and friends, and his sisters, who are great cooks, took care of the food. We were married in a chapel, and there was a mariachi. My family was appalled by the whole thing. It didn't matter that I was pregnant; they still thought I was crazy to get married. As my sisters pointed out—minutes before we walked into the chapel—when they tried to talk me out of going through with the marriage, Marcos and I were very different. My parents were so opposed to the marriage that they decided not to attend the wedding. Once again, my hope was that everything would work out, and they would come around and accept Marcos, and we would all live happily ever after.

Trouble from the Beginning

I think one of the biggest problems Marcos and I faced is that we had different ideas about male/female roles in a marriage. Marcos wanted a stay-at-home wife who focused on cooking and cleaning and making her husband happy. He was very honest about this. As soon as I got pregnant and moved in with him, he made his wishes and expectations clear: He would be the sole breadwinner. I had always worked and earned a living—I had been financially independent since I was a teenager. It was difficult for me to give up my independence. Nonetheless, I complied and immediately stopped working for my parents as well as doing makeup for clients.

Marcos also wanted me to become more conservative and subdued about my appearance. He didn't want me to wear makeup or jewelry, preferring to see me in clothing in which I was completely covered up—long skirts, long sleeves, and high necklines. If he had his way, there would be no more manicures or pedicures in this girl's life.

There was another big problem that kept presenting itself: Marcos had a tough time dealing with the fact that there had been other men in my life before him, something he never mentioned before I got pregnant. At first, I guess I was flattered by his jealousy, which I confused for passion. But I would come to find his attitude and actions scary and controlling. I remember an early argument that took place on my birthday. I had gone out of my way to look my best;

I had my hair done and put on a pretty outfit. When Marcos arrived home, he misinterpreted what I was doing and was furious. As far as Marcos was concerned, if I wore makeup, it was a sign that I was cheating on him; if I showed cleavage, I was a slut. He accused me of trying to look good for somebody else, called me horrible, degrading names, and stormed off. I guess he then thought about the cruel things he said and started to feel guilty, because he quickly returned with a mariachi. He did this kind of emotional turnaround often. I accepted it, and it became the norm. This time, when he and the mariachi all arrived, I was still crying. I must have been a sight: a newly pregnant woman, barely restraining her emotions—a confusing combination of heartbreak, rage, and disappointment—trying to smile and listen to a serenade of "Bésame Mucho."

I Was Afraid of Another Failed Relationship

I probably should have left Marcos at the first sign that he was abusive. But I didn't. I had never experienced anything like that, and it shocked and surprised me. I started believing everything he told me about myself. It was the first time I was exposed to this level of psychological as well as physical abuse.

By getting married, I realized that I had messed up big time. I was frequently inundated by a torrent of different emotions, thoughts, and concerns. I was too embarrassed to tell my parents the truth about what was going on—and once again, I felt as if I had let them down. I was so afraid of hearing their reactions. I was also really concerned about what other people would say about me. And once again, I was afraid of being alone. But more than that, I was afraid of Marcos's explosive temperament. How would he react if I tried to leave? The fact that I was pregnant played a large role in all my concerns. I didn't want to give birth alone, again, and I certainly didn't want to be alone for the rest of my life. But would I ever find another man who wanted to be with a woman with three children and such a demonstrably rocky personal history? Thoughts like these tumbled around in my head.

So I tried; I really tried to be the kind of wife Marcos wanted. I wanted the marriage to work, and I was determined to do everything in my power to make that happen. If I did everything he wanted the way he wanted it, would he become less angry? If that meant that I would never wear makeup and always wear outfits that make me look as though I belonged in another century, that's what I did. If that meant that I would stop working, give up my career as well as my sense of independence, I went along with the program. And if that meant that I had to learn to cook, I cooked. When we dated, Marcos gave me roses and stuffed animals. Once we were married, he gave me stuff for the house—pots and pans and a tortilla maker.

At least some of our problems revolved around my not being a good cook. I'm going to repeat once again that I was a sh*tty cook. I couldn't make a muffin without it coming out looking deformed. With Marcos, I tried to learn to cook. Honest. But it didn't always work out the way I wanted. I might also add that Marcos frequently compared my cooking unfavorably to that of his sisters—two good women who basically tried very hard to be kind to me, so I don't want to blame them for Marcos's culinary demands. But it felt as though nothing I did pleased him. My coffee, for example, was always off—not enough cinnamon or too much cinnamon being common complaints.

And then there was the big pozole fiasco. Pozole is a soup-like Mexican stew. The main ingredient is hominy, which is mixed with meat, usually pork, and a variety of intricately prepared vegetables. It's a complicated dish for someone who can barely scramble an egg. But Marcos kept telling me how much he loved pozole, and I, wanting to meet his standards for being a good wife, decided I would try making it for him. I had always heard that the way to a man's heart is through his stomach. Could I ease the tension in our relationship by making one of his favorite dishes? Maybe then he would see how hard I was trying.

Pozole requires a variety of different steps. The hominy, for example, should be soaked and boiled and simmered for an hour. In fact, something special has to be done to just about every ingredient, including the chilies, which need to be blended and pureed. But I truly wanted to please him, so I called my mother and asked, "How do I make pozole?"

My mother gave me instructions, and I was off and running. I was a woman on a mission, so I spent a huge amount of time and thought shopping for the correct ingredients and then, most of a morning, chopping, blending, and braising before stewing and simmering the whole thing for even more hours. After I was finished, it took me at least an hour to clean the kitchen. When Marcos came home, I proudly presented him with the pozole.

"What's this?" he asked with a sneer. "Pozole is supposed to be green. This is red! I'm not eating this sh*t," he said as he angrily threw the bowl of pozole against a wall.

Nobody had told me that there are different kinds of pozole—red, green, and clear—each connected to a different part of Mexico. My mother had given me a recipe for her red pozole. When Marcos's sisters made pozole, it turned out green. Now I know. But then I didn't.

While I scraped pozole off the wall and floor, Marcos called his sister. "Guess what Rosie did?" he said. "She tried to make pozole, and she didn't make it green."

I didn't take Marcos's complaints well. I was a pregnant woman with swollen ankles who had spent a day standing on her feet chopping and stirring.

The longer we were together, the more insulting and abusive Marcos became—often calling me names, putting me down, and making fun of my weight. Thinking back, I don't know why I accepted what I accepted. I found his insults emotionally abusive and scarring. I will never forget shyly confiding my dreams of being able to work on television. Marcos immediately erupted with laughter. "Are you crazy?" he asked. "Who would hire you for something like that? You're too old and too fat. Get over it!" If I talked about trying to lose weight, Marcos would respond by telling me that it was never going to happen—I was always going to be fat and ugly.

And then there was the drinking. Marcos would sometimes go out in the evening and come back angry and belligerent, calling me names and reeking of the smell of whiskey, beer, and cigarettes. When that happened, I hated being around him. One night when

I was almost seven months pregnant, he arrived home angry and full of insults. He pushed me against a wall, and I was crying. He was so angry and resentful toward me, and I didn't understand why. Why didn't he love me? I did everything he asked. Why did he hate me? After he fell asleep, I found that he had coins from the Bunny Ranch, the well-known Las Vegas legal brothel, in his boot. In what was almost a replay of what happened with both Gianni and Anthony, there were too many nights when Marcos didn't come home. To make it even worse, when he did come home, he was insulting and mean, slamming doors, throwing phones, grabbing my arm so hard that there would be bruises that I would have to conceal from my parents by lying. His anger was terrifying. In the morning, of course, he would be apologetic and say he remembered nothing about what happened. Sometimes he would even bring me flowers. It felt as though I was married to two different people.

Once again, I was very pregnant and very beaten down. But I was determined not to be completely dependent on an unfaithful man. Infidelity has always been my tipping point. I absolutely knew I had to get past my fears of being alone. If I didn't, something made me feel as though I was going to die. I had so many chest pains I didn't know what was going to happen. This had gone beyond being a bad relationship. This was toxic and dangerous. And at least I had the name of a good private investigator. When I called the investigator, he was genuinely shocked and upset that it was me. "Please," he said, "tell me that you're only calling to say hello and to ask how I am doing? Please, honey, don't tell me you got married again."

What would the investigator find out? Well, it didn't take long for him to learn that Marcos was having an affair with a secretary in Vegas. It was very similar to what happened with Anthony. Same story, different secretary. The investigator gave me all the proof I needed—including tapes as well as photographs. When the investigator told me what he found out, my major reaction was embarrassment and an all-too-familiar sense of shame. Here I was, once again, in a bad relationship—once again pregnant, and once again seeking the services of a PI. I couldn't help asking myself, What the f*ck is wrong with me? Will I ever get anything right?

When Marcos came home that night, I was looking at the television.

"What are you watching?" he asked.

"It's interesting," I replied. "Come, take a look."

When he saw the photographs of himself with the woman, Marcos didn't know what to say. I was silent for a few minutes, and then I lost it. Up until that point, every time Marcos had done or said something mean, hurtful, or insulting to me, I had stayed quiet. Because I had wanted this relationship to work and I didn't want to create problems, I had stayed quiet for all his abuse. I always did what he said and never complained. Well, I no longer wanted the relationship. I desperately wanted out. Everything that had happened between us came to a head, and I went batsh*t crazy screaming and throwing things around the house. It was as though I had to do this as a way of making up for my many months of silence. Marcos, who had never before seen me like that, just stood there watching his stuff being flung around the room. I was out of control, and I think he was stunned by my anger. Finally, he walked out.

At the first hint of daylight, I packed up Bella, Valentino, and our belongings and it was over. Self-preservation was a greater motivating factor than fear.

Alex was born two weeks later.

Don't Let Fear Become Your GPS

Every single one of us knows what it means to be scared—and sometimes it feels as though there are many, many reasons in life to be frightened. Personally, as a young woman, I had my own list of fears. I was afraid of not being able to support my children; I was afraid of being alone forever. And that's just for starters. Sometimes fear is paralyzing; sometimes it makes us do things we otherwise wouldn't.

Of course, we all also make mistakes. Frequently the biggest mistakes we make come about because we have allowed our fears to guide us. When we are being guided by fear, we don't make the right choices or take the right chances. And sometimes, because we are afraid, we jump into situations that are as stupid as they are painful. By so doing, we hope we will achieve some respite from our biggest fears. It doesn't work that way. In my case, jumping from relationship to relationship because I was afraid of being alone is a huge error that dominated much of my life. And let's admit it. I also stayed in relationships because I was also afraid of what people would say if I left. I felt ashamed and was concerned that I would be criticized and judged for walking down this path again. Even if they didn't say anything, would people always look at me as though there was something broken about me? It goes without saying that I was also afraid of the unknown.

My mom always told me, "Walk by faith and trust that you will be guided!" There comes a time in life when, no matter how scared you feel, you have to stop being so fearful of the unknown and have faith that something better is going to happen. Otherwise fear can turn into a kind of negative prayer waiting to happen. Don't let your fears motivate you into accepting situations that you know, in your gut, are more than a little flawed, not to mention potentially dangerous. Instead, put out what you want to happen. Have faith in your future and what you deserve. Be courageous enough to stand by what you want.

We all need to stand our ground and make our decisions based not on our fears but on our deepest beliefs and convictions—on solid faith, not foolish fear. Have patience and be prepared to wait for the love you deserve.

Change your GPS, and take a leap of faith. These are moments when you learn who you are, discover your strengths, and realize how far you can stretch yourself. These are our growing moments.

Tell yourself: I am faithfully guided!

I will overcome all adversity and create powerful change in my life.

> *Now faith is the assurance of things hoped for,*
> *the conviction of things not seen.*
>
> HEBREWS 11:1 (ESV)

CHAPTER 8

Put Your Sh*t Out There

WORK HAS ALWAYS BEEN AN ESSENTIAL PART OF MY LIFE. Even if we ended up choosing our own different careers, my father wanted his children to know the family business from the ground up. Starting as a teenager, I did it all: sales, hiring, firing, contracts, as well as being out in the yard managing drivers, not to mention serving as my dad's "bad cop," working in collections and keeping finances straight.

My father's business was always my financial fallback position, and after my daughter was born, I knew there was no fooling around. I had to support my daughter and arrived at the office every morning bright and early. But I also had another source of income—the makeup business I started in high school, something my entrepreneurial family had always encouraged. When Bella was about a year old, out of the blue, an old client asked if I would be able to do makeup for an event. Why not? I had continued to read beauty magazines to stay on top of the trends, practicing on myself, and I had always kept my makeup kit fresh and ready. On the day of the event, I packed up my supplies and my daughter and headed off. It was the first and last time I took baby Bella with me for a job. My usually well-behaved baby girl, who was just starting to walk, kept getting into everything. From that day forward, making sure that sitters and nannies or my parents were there to take care of my children became one of my first priorities.

Most of my makeup work came from referrals and word of mouth. My initial business plan was focused on individual women who wanted to look their best for a specific event. Then, I began to think more about the events themselves—doing makeup for entire bridal parties, for example. Before long, I had a steady stream of parties, events, and, yes, many weddings. Doing makeup for all those weddings could be emotionally challenging. Not only was I hired to make the bride and her party as beautiful as possible, I was also expected to be supportive and cheerful, which was sometimes the most difficult part of my job. I had to make certain that any general feelings of loneliness and unhappiness I was experiencing didn't bubble to the surface. I was there to help couples celebrate love and marriage. But after my relationships fell apart, I would watch happy brides with a sense of deep cynicism and think to myself, I wonder how long that is going to last? And I sometimes couldn't help but feel at least a little bit sorry for myself. I honestly didn't think that romantic love would ever again be part of my life. Looking at a happy bride, I couldn't help but feel a little bit jealous. Why was she smiling so much, and what did she know—that I didn't—about love and maintaining relationships?

Another recurring question was often present in the back of my mind: "What is wrong with me?" I didn't think about whether this was a self-protective, positive, or healthy question; yet as I worked on makeup for wedding parties, I kept hearing my inner voice questioning my very essence.

And then, there were the bridezillas—young, beautiful women who were amazingly narcissistic and stunningly self-involved. I remember one bride in particular who began screaming at me and her mother, who she said looked "too old and too fat" to be seen standing near the bride. She expected me to tape her mother's neck so she didn't appear to have a double chin. Of course, many other brides and their families were lovely and kind. I would look at women who were so much in love and so eager to begin married life that I would want to cry. I hoped and prayed that they would continue to enjoy happiness, even though I personally didn't always believe it would happen.

As the makeup business began to flourish, I started getting more commercial calls to do trade shows, which typically use many models; I frequently had to hire a team of other makeup artists to work with me. Many of my jobs would entail my going to the casinos and nightclubs, which I always found a little bit traumatic. I once had a job at a nightclub, and when I got there with my makeup kit, the gatekeeper, a bouncer who must have been about six-five, wouldn't let me in because I didn't fit the look they wanted.

"We're full. Move on," he said.

"You don't understand," I kept explaining, "I'm not here to attend the event—I'm here to do makeup." I was finally able to phone somebody, who came out to tell the bouncer to let me in, but it was totally humiliating.

Problems of a Single Mom

For a brief period of time, while I was married to Marcos, I stopped working, but after our marriage ended, there I was with three young children to support. Working as a makeup artist, which meant standing on my feet for hours, was very labor intensive, and I was spending a small fortune on babysitters. My problem: finding a way to create an income stream that was less exhausting while also making it possible for me to spend more time with the children. Creating my own private-label cosmetic line was an obvious business choice. I started with very few products: moisturizers, powders, eye shadows, glosses, and shimmers. Most of my products were from companies that created cosmetics for private-label companies like mine, but I made my own shimmers, which were always my best sellers.

My elegant mom was always there to advise me on packaging: "You want your product to be good, but you also want it to look beautiful." My entrepreneurial father was also there with advice, encouraging me to think about expanding and growing my business. I was grateful to my family and friends for their support in starting a cosmetics business. Lily always helped me, and Genesis jumped in to help put labels on the cosmetics. The biggest challenge I faced was finding a place to sell my products.

This is a common problem in Las Vegas and there is a common solution—head for the swap meets, which are huge. A swap meet is a place where people congregate to sell, buy, or sometimes even trade all kinds of products, ranging from electronic equipment and automobile parts to clothing and furniture, both used and new. Music is usually playing, and there are always vendors selling food. Many swap meets are outdoors, but others are sheltered and in well-established locations where vendors can rent individual enclosed spaces.

I rented an attractive space, and during the day on weekends, I packed up the kids, the strollers, the carriers, the cosmetics, and my makeup kit and headed for the swap meet, where we were surrounded by hundreds of other booths that had been rented by various businesses of all kinds—fabrics, clothing, jewelry, kitchen equipment, and even fortune-telling. Once there, I would do makeup demonstrations and makeovers for people interested in buying cosmetics. It was exhausting.

And Still Not Making Enough Money

That's when I decided to launch a campaign to expand my cosmetics business. To do that, I needed professional photographs for advertising and publicity. I decided to talk first with my friend, well-known fashion photographer Oscar Picazo; I had been lucky enough to meet him when I was doing makeup for some of his shoots. My original plan was to hire a model, but when I talked to Oscar and expressed my concerns about the cost, he suggested that I could be my own model: "All the photographs are going to be from the neck up, and you have a beautiful face. Save your money. We'll take pictures of you." He was so kind. I had no way of knowing that Oscar's words would change my life. At the time I thought, Saving money sounds good.

Even so, the idea of having professional photos taken of me was scary. Today, if you do a search of my name on the internet, you will see hundreds of photos of me in every conceivable kind of clothing and pose. But until that moment, there were perhaps a little more than a dozen photos of me, taken throughout my entire life and hidden away in my house where nobody could see them. I had always avoided all photo ops. As a child and adolescent, I had been traumatized by school picture days and have no idea what happened to the results. I think my mom had some pictures of me taken when I was three, but that was about it. A few other photos were taken at major life moments, such as my high school graduation and Quinceañera and when I got married. Because I didn't want anyone looking at my body, I made sure photographs of me were few and far between.

But I decided to be brave about the photos and trust Oscar, who told me to relax—only my perfectly made-up face would be seen, and he was sure I would like what I saw.

I knew intuitively that I would be too nervous to do my own makeup, so I asked a terrific Las Vegas makeup artist and friend, Zee, to do both my hair and makeup. I had no idea what was going to happen next, but I went along with the program.

When I showed up for the shoot, I was such a nervous wreck that I was kind of brain dead. Oscar, who is incredibly creative, posed me in a variety of different positions and backgrounds so we could get different looks. Until that moment, I had no realistic idea of how difficult it is to model. Oscar positioned me lying down, standing up, and scrunched up. For one shot, he had me lying on my side, sort of balanced on my knees. I thought I would never be able to get up. For another, he had me stand like I was hovering over something. I remember he told me to hold my neck out as far as possible and hold my breath.

Well, Oscar, who always takes amazingly wonderful photographs, took some amazingly wonderful photographs of me. When I saw them, I couldn't believe my eyes. Who was that girl? I had never thought of myself as being seen in that light. As far as I was concerned, it certainly didn't look like the me I imagined myself to be. For the first time in my life, I looked at photographs of myself and felt happy doing so. Oscar posted them in various places on the internet, including Facebook. So did I.

They went viral!

Suddenly I had phone calls from major modeling agencies like Wilhelmina asking for full-body shots. When I complied and sent them what they wanted, the responses I received were of the "Stop messing with us" variety. They were reluctant to believe that my four-hundred-pound plus-size body went with Oscar's photos of my face. Agencies that started out by sending me multiple emails telling me how excited they were by my face never responded to my body shots. I was, as they say, ghosted. Despite these reactions, I began to learn more about the world of plus-size modeling. I was more than curious. In the realm of possibility, was this something I could do?

An Investment of Time, Money, and Energy

A friend suggested that I might start out by competing for the title of Miss Nevada Plus. "Plus" meant that I didn't have to be thin! That was encouraging. I don't know where I got the courage, but this was very much a "Why not?" moment in my life. Once I decided that this was a possible goal, I was committed, so I did everything required, filling out all the forms and getting endorsements. And I won! Let me be totally honest here. I think I may have won because I was the only applicant who filled out all the forms and fulfilled all the requirements. But it didn't matter. I was determined to succeed, and I was heading to Nationals!

After years of listening to people talk about the size of my hips, I decided that, if nothing else, I not only wanted to be Miss Plus America, I deserved it. Who could be more "Plus" than me? At this point, my incredibly competitive spirit kicked in. If I was going to do this, I was going to do it right. I did a lot of research, which showed me that I would have to do more than just show up with a full figure. I would need outfits for the various categories, such as "evening gown." There was, thank God, no bathing suit competition, but there was a competition for "elegant pant wear." And there was a talent competition. I wasn't able to sing or play the flute, but there were possible substitute categories. One was titled Fashion Runway Modeling—I decided that would be my talent.

I could do this—but I was going to need help in the form of a runway coach.

Don't Wobble

My runway coach, Christina, was a beautiful model—tall and thin. We spoke first on the phone, and I told her who I was and what I wanted to do. Nonetheless when I showed up at her door, I think she was shocked by my size. When we started working together, I think she was also more than surprised that I basically knew nothing about modeling. But twice a week for six weeks, I showed up and she taught me the fundamentals of runway modeling and a few other things as well.

"Where's your modeling bag?" she asked me.

"Huh?" I answered.

Turns out a modeling bag is an essential. Among other things, it contains several pairs of shoes, including flats and high heels, along with a selection of different undergarments, such as thongs (white, beige, black) that will fit under different kinds of clothing. This was a first, because until that time, I exclusively wore granny panties. Models also carry body shapers such as Spanx to help smooth out their curves.

I remember Christina suggesting that I start out by getting a full-body wax. I tried to point out to her that I was close to four hundred hefty pounds. No way I was going to be comfortable showing anybody—even a waxing aesthetician—my hoo-ha.

This whole process was giving me an education. Christina and I would watch videos of pageants—like Miss America. "Watch how graceful this contestant looks when she turns," she would say. At the time I wasn't thinking about grace. I was mostly worried about walking in high heels without falling over.

And then Christina would have me walk and pose, saying, "This is how you should stand to look longer and thinner."

Christina's attitude sometimes made me laugh. When talking about my body, nobody else had ever used the expression "longer and thinner."

But the main focus of our work together was "walking" in heels.

"Please don't wobble," Christina would say over and over and over again. I would finally stop wobbling, but then I might start to sway my hips as I walked. "You're swaying," Christina would remind me.

Christina introduced me to posing, walking, and turning onstage, as well as relaxing my body and being able to look at the audience and speak publicly. At my weight, turning in heels and walking down the runway was incredibly difficult. I practiced with Christina, and I practiced at home. "Walk, breathe, and stand straight" became my mantra. Christina went so far as to put a cinnamon stick in my bra, positioned so that if I slouched, I would receive an immediate poke.

What Will I Wear?

It was impossible to find outfits, even in stores specializing in clothing for larger women, and I sure didn't want to end up wearing something that resembled a tent. My mom always had her clothes made by a wonderful Las Vegas seamstress named Larissa, a kind and nonjudgmental woman who took on the project of making me a few beautiful outfits, including a hot-pink-and-black dress and a blue formal gown with a train. The dresses were beaded and glamorous and required yards and yards of fabric. I was struggling financially, so I was painfully aware of the cost. One of the dresses, which I wore onstage for a total of three minutes, cost close to $2,500. In order to pay for it, I needed to do even more makeup jobs. I still remember how hard I busted my ass to pay for that dress.

When I started my journey to the Miss Plus America pageant, I think most of my family questioned my sanity. Actually, they thought I was nuts. However, they were also happy to see me energized and with a goal, as opposed to making appointments to see doctors or sitting home crying on the couch. I was enthusiastic, and I was committed; for the most part, they did whatever they could to support me. My parents, for example, agreed to stay home with my sons. It was a two-day drive to Lafayette, Louisiana, and when I loaded the car with my outfits, my exceptional team—my brother, my sister-in-law, and a makeup and hair stylist—piled in with me. I also took my ten-year-old daughter, Bella.

A Liberating Experience—No More Hiding Out

Seeing the other contestants together was a transformative experience. For the very first time in my life, I didn't feel as though I was alone. Realizing there was a community of large beautiful women was a total mind f*ck! Seeing all those women together may have been one of the most exciting and empowering things that has ever happened to me. I didn't know there were that many confident plus-size women in the country. It was astonishing to me—a major aha! moment. All these beautiful large women with big heels, big hair, big lashes, and big jewelry joyfully and proudly walking around made me want to cry with happiness.

I had been avoiding doing anything that brought attention to my body for my entire life—always hiding out, choosing clothing that served one primary function: covering me up. At Miss Plus America, I realized I didn't have to do that anymore. I watched my fellow contestants prancing around and came to the conclusion that I could prance around with the best of them. It was time for me to reveal who I was and start enjoying myself. I could wear high heels, show my arms, embrace my body, and have a great time being me. What a mind-boggling realization!

Just as important was watching my daughter react to all the women. I think my daughter, like me, became empowered by the experience of being a part of a larger community of beautiful women. One of the events of the week was a pajama party for women, and I took Bella with me. I saw her eyes widen and open up to the possibilities of life. When we returned home, I also noticed that she began participating in more activities at school.

What Happened?

Well, I won things: I won Miss People's Choice, and I won an award for my runway work, where I was in pain from my high heels, but I absolutely didn't wobble. *National Geographic,* which had a film crew there, seemed to be convinced that I was going to win the competition, because they followed me throughout the pageant, and ultimately I was featured in an episode of their television series *Taboo.*

I also actually thought I had a good shot at winning the pageant. But I didn't. I didn't even place in the top ten. Was I devastated? Not really. I was still so high from the entire experience and everything

I had learned about myself and the world that I remained energized and inspired.

Most important: I had a new attitude about myself and the possibilities that existed for my future. And I was determined. When I stood on the stage at Miss Plus America, I found a new piece of me—a part of me came to life for the first time.

A Promise to Myself: I Would Stop Hiding Out

After a lifetime of covering up and hiding out under baggy clothing, I made a major decision: I was going to wear clothing that exposed my arms, my legs, and, yes, my cleavage. I was going to put myself out there and I was going to be proud of who I was and how I looked.

It's an interesting question: Can changing what you wear change the way you approach life? Most women would probably answer yes to that question. We realize that intuitively we hide behind our outfits. We all have a look that we favor, and when most of us open our closets, we see outfit after outfit, all resembling one another. My closets all featured clothing that hid my body. I vowed all that was going to change.

My new and very strong decision: I was going to accept my body, and I was going to show the world that I was a proud plus-size woman. And I was going to try to make a living doing just that—by being a plus-size model.

As far as I was concerned, the time had come. I told myself, You have nothing to lose—the time has come to just put your sh*t out there.

Fulfilling a "Crazy" Dream: Make a Plan

When I returned from the pageant, I got together with Oscar Picazo, and we started creating a portfolio of photographs of me wearing clothing that didn't even attempt to hide my body. There were no more dark and oversize long-sleeved tents in my life. I wore bright colors, high heels and short-sleeved tops and shorter skirts that showed my calves. I remember one set of fabulous photos in which Oscar posed me wearing a lovely outfit next to a very muscular man, naked from the waist up. It was a study in contrasts.

I created a website, www.RosieMercado.com, which featured my photographs along with a bio. And both Oscar and I posted the photos on our Facebook pages. Once again, we received tons of likes, loves, and shares. I loved all the responses, but they weren't getting me the work I needed. What could I do to generate a real modeling career?

When I told people I wanted to become a model, many of them laughed. They told me it was a crazy dream and I should get real. Here's something I want you to know: The world is full of naysayers who will do nothing to help you get where you want to go. Avoid them. If you want to talk about your dreams, do so only with those few people who will support you. Always try to surround yourself with people who will help you grow. Once you achieve your goals, the same people who criticized your dreams will be there to congratulate you and tell you that they always knew how much you were going to accomplish.

It's time to stop talking and make a plan.

Stop Talking About Your Dreams and Start Living Them Out

> *A dream written down with a date becomes a goal. A goal broken down into steps becomes a plan. A plan backed by action makes your dreams come true.*

I have that quote by businessman and author Greg Reid memorized. It's a great one for all of us to remember. So, write down your dream and put a date next to it. Now you have more than a dream; you have a goal.

The next thing to do is create a step-by-step plan. Make the decision that each day you will do at least one thing that brings you closer to fulfilling your dream. The first thing you can do, for example, is carve out at least an hour a day to work toward your goal. If you want to be an artist, buy the supplies you need and spend an hour creating. If you want to be an actor, sign up for a class and follow through. If you want to be a writer, spend at least an hour a day working on a story. If you have a simple goal, such as "I wish I could have organized closets," commit to spending time each day organizing your closets and stop wishing. If you want to lose weight, get a meal plan together, sign up for an exercise class, or make a plan to walk for an hour each day. We all have goals and dreams—some of them appear very large, while others seem very small. Whatever your dreams, you need to start taking the small steps that will help you get where you want to be. Make the firm determination that you will follow through and explore any avenue that leads you to the place you want to go. It takes perseverance, faith, action, and consistency—the keys to success.

Also know what you are willing to give up in order to get where you want to be. There is always a trade-off. Almost inevitably you will have to give up something from your old life in order to move ahead and get a new one. Don't be afraid to do this.

Stop waiting for right circumstances before you move forward toward your new life. And don't wait for anybody else to give you permission. You don't need anybody else's permission but your own. So give yourself that permission and start building the momentum you need. Tell yourself: This is my dream; this is my truth; and start moving.

The Face of Full Figured Fashion Week

A friend told me about Full Figured Fashion Week and suggested I apply. Taking place in New York City, it was a week that focused on fashion and plus-size women. And there was a contest! They would choose a plus-size woman to represent the plus-size industry. It seemed like a perfect opportunity to get some exposure for myself, and I desperately wanted to win.

The Face of Full Figured Fashion Week was decided by online votes. My challenge would be to find a way to convince lots and lots of people to take the time to go to the correct website to vote. And then of course to vote for me.

Once I decided that I was going to apply, I made a commitment to do whatever I could to convince people to vote for me. I knew that I needed to be shameless in getting those votes. This was no time to be shy! Not only did I contact everyone I knew, I created flyers, and I walked through malls and office buildings in Las Vegas. I needed those votes. Someone introduced me to a well-known internet personality named Skyy John, an actor who regularly interviewed a wide variety of people—and then posted the interviews on YouTube. Skyy John interviewed me. The interview, which asked people to vote for me, was called "The Hottest Fat Chick Ever!?!" Lots and lots of people viewed the interview, and at least a few of them must have voted for me. In fact, I got tons of votes from Skyy John's interview, and I was so grateful.

It all worked. I received the most votes. When I got the call that I would be the next Face of Full Figured Fashion Week, I was stunned. When I thought about what had happened to me, a shy, divorced, plus-size Mexican American mother, I was shocked. I sat in my chair staring into space for a full thirty minutes, trying to figure out the ramifications of what I had just done and what it meant for my life. This was definitely a first: Not only was I going to New York City—someone else was going to be paying for my flight. Unbelievable!

This Was My Chance, and I Took It

It was the first time that I had ever won anything, let alone something this big, and my excitement was through the roof. Other than learning that I had won, I didn't know much about what was going to happen or what I should do. But I knew that I was going to get to walk a runway in New York. This was the real deal! I was determined to be fearless about making the most of this opportunity and launching my career. As far as I was concerned, there would be no more hiding out in bathroom stalls trying to avoid people staring at me. Now I had a completely different approach.

LOOK AT ME! I am beautiful. It was the first time I was able to verbalize that thought.

When was the last time you looked in a mirror and said, "I am beautiful!"? Practice doing this every day, and be aware of the difference it makes in how you feel about yourself. You are beautiful!

I was in New York for a week, staying at a hotel. Everyone was amazingly kind, and I got to walk an extraordinary white runway wearing beautiful clothing. I knew this was my opportunity. If I didn't make the most of it, I would be returning home with nothing to show from this experience except a few good photographs.

I was scared out of my wits, but I was a woman on a mission. It was Full Figured Fashion Week, and I knew that most of the designers of plus-size clothing for women would be there. I made sure I knew who they were and where they would be standing. Whenever I had the opportunity to talk to one of them, I grabbed it. I must have spoken to at least five designers. I started out by introducing myself and quickly moved forward with my pitch.

"You know," I would start out, "there are great opportunities in the plus-size market.

"Many of the women in this market are larger than a size sixteen, but currently clothing is not designed for these larger sizes. All these women also want beautiful clothing. As a model, I would like to be one of the first to represent these women. These women need to see what the clothing they are buying actually looks like on a woman who, like me, is their size."

I explained to each of the designers something they already knew. The clothing being designed for plus-size women didn't really reflect the actual size of most women. Why were they not designing clothing for larger women—women like me?

Approaching each of the designers and describing my vision took a lot of courage. When I talked about the plight of larger women, I was talking from my soul. I had spent my life hiding out. I was so often called ugly because of the size of my hips. I knew I wasn't the only woman who felt that way. We all needed help. Beautiful clothing designed especially for us was a wonderful first step.

My dad always taught me, "When you want something from somebody, you have to start by going up to them and asking." That's what I did. There was an afternoon event at which I spoke to all the designers, and I knew this might be my only chance to zero in and say what I wanted to say. It was now or never. As I moved from designer to designer, and they failed to show enthusiasm, in my head I said, *Next—move on.* Although they were all polite and gracious, I could see that my words weren't having the desired impact; most told me that this wasn't the direction in which they were heading. I didn't give up; I simply did not let all the "no" responses stop me. I just kept going. And then I began talking to the amazing and brilliant Yuliya Raquel, who at the time was a designer at IGIGI.

As I started to speak, I could see that my words were resonating with her. I told her my dream. I wanted to be part of a campaign that would inspire larger women to buy lovely clothing and be happy with how they looked. Many larger women don't really see themselves as beautiful. They have all been criticized for their weight, and they are not accustomed to thinking of themselves as beautiful or powerful.

Yuliya Raquel and IGIGI gave me my first campaign. The "I Am Beautiful" campaign launched at Full Figured Fashion Week in the spring of 2011, and it featured a video of me describing what it felt like to have people call you ugly because of your size and then reaffirming that "I Am Beautiful."

Part of the launch was a collection of extraordinarily gorgeous bridal gowns going up to size 34. Suddenly I had work—real modeling jobs that paid real money. IGIGI's "I Am Beautiful" campaign launched my career for real and changed my life.

And I Had a Larger Goal

By then, my goals had changed. I genuinely wanted to be able to help larger women find beautiful clothing. For me, the experience of shopping always ranged from nightmare to traumatic. I think my feelings about shopping for clothing are shared by most, if not all, plus-size women. I will never forget being twelve years old and wanting to shop at a store called Contempo Casuals. That was where the cool girls shopped. Why shouldn't I shop there too? I convinced my mother and headed off to the mall, all excited.

I still remember an outfit worn by the coolest girl in the school—flowered palazzo pants with a white T-shirt, accessorized with a black choker and a black bucket hat. That's what I wanted. When I got to the store, it goes without saying that I couldn't find pants or a T-shirt that fit. At that age, even though I had large hips, I wasn't anywhere near as big as I would later become, but at that time, few stores carried even minimally larger sizes. I ended up buying the bucket hat and the little black choker and feeling unbearably sad.

Back then, thinking about the girl in the palazzo pants, I felt deep and unhealthy envy. It was probably the first time I felt envy or jealousy, and I still remember the moment. It was probably intensified because the girl wore her outfit to school picture day, and I couldn't stop myself from having mean thoughts about how she looked. I told myself she looked ugly, which of course she didn't. On that school picture day, I probably felt particularly bad because I was wearing one of the few outfits my mother and I could find that fit—a pair of baggy white pants and a dark blue blazer with a little anchor logo on the lapel. I looked like a matron.

I can't tell you how much I always hated hearing the dreaded sentence "I'm sorry, but we don't carry any sizes that are large enough for you." Until recently, there were only a very few stores like Lane Bryant that carried plus-sizes. And even in these stores, sizes tended to stop at about 28. At my heaviest, I was much larger than a 28.

And then there were always the "helpful" salespeople who tried to get in a few words of "advice." I will always remember one salesperson in particular. She was tall, elegant, and very chic, wearing beautiful Chanel pearl earrings; she had a burgundy manicure, and her white hair was cut in a perfect bob.

"You have such a beautiful face, dear," she said. "You should take better care of yourself. Do you know how big you are?"

I wanted to reply, "No. Oh my God . . . Thank you for bringing it to my attention. I just looked in the store mirror and saw how big I am. What a shock. I never realized that I was fat. Wow. Thanks for telling me!"

When it comes to talking about weight, some people need to know the difference between empowering another woman and putting her down.

Yes, I Felt Proud

I completely identified with the problems that women who were larger than a size 16 experienced in terms of shopping for clothing. This was my world! Being part of a campaign to help larger women like me find beautiful clothing made me incredibly happy. In the blink of an eye, for many people, I became the face of the plus-size woman. Not only was I starting to get more work, I was developing an internet presence. Out of the blue, when I posted something on the internet, thousands of people were paying attention, and many responded. I was building a following. Until that moment, I really had no idea how strongly the message that plus-size women could be beautiful was resonating with so many women.

Put Your Sh*t Out There

If you want to create success in your life, you have to be fearless about moving forward. The process requires total determination. Make a plan, put one foot in front of the other, and just keep going. Failure is part of the equation—we will all have it in our lives. But you need to recognize that you are not going to get where you want to be on the first try. Expect that things will go wrong—realize that you will feel like giving up. But that is not an option. Don't allow yourself to be defeated by things that go wrong, and no matter what, just keep going.

We will always meet people who have negative things to say—that's one way the universe tests us to see how badly we want our dreams. Just remember that it's always our choice whether to let negativity into our lives. Don't get offended by every criticism or nonbeliever you encounter. Just stay focused on your dream and find your reward in the work. When you step into the energy of creating, you will attract those teachers, mentors, and opportunities that align with your heart's dreams and desires.

And don't be shy about asking for help. It doesn't matter what you are trying to achieve—whether it's weight loss, a more satisfying career, going back to school, or creating a more beautiful and organized living space—you may need help or advice. Do your research, and organize your support system. You have to start somewhere. If you want to reach your destination, building momentum is your first goal.

Put yourself and your goals out there, and don't be embarrassed or ashamed if people make fun of what you want. Just start. Getting to where you want to go is like putting a jigsaw puzzle together. Start by putting down the first piece. Search for the next one. If you get it wrong, say to yourself, "Next." Just keep going: "Next. Next. Next." If you knock on the wrong door and you get turned down, just say, "Next," and keep on going.

If you feel as though you are failing, stop asking yourself, "What's wrong with me?" I had to learn to stop asking myself that question. Instead I learned to ask myself, *Why do I feel this way?* In my case, I had allowed unhealthy relationships and experiences to define who I was. I had to realize that these were merely relationships and experiences that happened in my past. They had little or nothing to do with my essential essence.

Just keep heading toward your goals. When you start actually moving in the direction you want to be heading, there is a sense of creativity and inspiration that gives you momentum and helps you go forward. You will look happier, and people will notice. And don't be afraid of messing up. Expect that it's going to happen, but don't let that dissuade you. Messing up gives you another opportunity to get closer to success. It teaches you what doesn't work. Becoming more aware of your mistakes is a sure sign that you are getting close to success. Keep moving and looking for the next door. Learn from your mistakes. I remember when I first learned to dance in high heels. I kept falling down. This was part of my process. Stop looking at failure as a bad thing. It's part of the success process. Whatever you want to learn and wherever you want to be, don't be afraid. Continue to take wise, informed risks, and keep moving in the direction you want to go.

Remember, spoken words are a prayer to the universe so make sure you speak life into your present and your future. Walk by faith and not by sight. Powerful dreams inspire powerful action!

CHAPTER 9

Discover What You Can Create for Yourself

AFTER MY SCARE WITH THE BRAIN CYST, AND WITH THREE horribly disappointing relationships behind me, I continued on a tremendous roller coaster with my weight. I was so determined to get healthy but still had been unsuccessful with getting off, and keeping off, the pounds.

I was waiting to get on the red-eye from Las Vegas to New York City, where I was scheduled to shoot an episode of *Curvy Girls,* a television reality show about plus-size models that I'd been shooting for about six months. Because I wanted to look my best, I was wearing a favorite outfit—a high-waisted skirt and a cute black-and-white-striped top

I designed myself, re-created from one I had seen in a fashion magazine. My shoes—four-inch-high open-toe platforms—were probably the most eye-catching part of the outfit. Hey, I was on my way to New York City, and I needed to look trendy! I had been through some tough times, but my life was definitely on the upswing, and at that moment, I was feeling pretty positive about myself and the path I was on.

As soon as the announcement came that the flight was about to board, my fellow passengers started to form a line. I had already organized my little carry-on and was heading for the line when out of the corner of my eye I spotted one of the boarding attendants walking in my direction.

He confronted me by saying, "Excuse me, but you need to purchase a second seat."

"What?" I replied. For a moment I was genuinely confused.

"You won't fit in one seat." He separated the words as he slowly repeated himself. "You-need-to-purchase-a-second-seat." He sounded almost punitive. "If you don't want this to happen again," he continued, "you always need to be sure that you have *two* seats." He emphasized the word "two." His tone of voice was neither discreet nor kind.

I was so taken aback that I started crying. Thinking about it now, I realize that I shouldn't have been all that surprised. I knew that I was definitely too big to fit into some cars. I knew that I couldn't go on amusement park rides with my children because the seats were too small. When I went into a new restaurant, I always subtly checked to make sure the chairs would be strong enough to hold my weight. I guess on some level I always worried that something like this could happen, but it still came as a shock—a harsh, emotional body blow so strong that it left me reeling.

As the tears started flowing down my face, I could see a small group of guys traveling together staring at me and laughing at my plight. Did one of them actually say, "She is one big bitch," or did I imagine it because I was so accustomed to hearing this kind of reaction to the way my body looked?

All I wanted to do was run home, a safe place, where I could hide under my covers and avoid the outside world, but that wasn't an option. I had no choice! The story I told myself to keep going was that I was a divorced woman with three young children to support and I absolutely had to get to New York for work, so I focused on drying my tears and quietly hurried off to purchase a second ticket, struggling not to sob and draw further attention to myself.

Once I got on the plane, the flight attendant was very kind, almost as if she felt the need to compensate for my embarrassment. Despite her gentle demeanor, I felt unbearably shamed, particularly when she placed a small sign on the seat next to me that read, SEAT TAKEN. It made everything so much more obvious.

Just numb it out, I told myself. Block it out and read your magazine. But that was easier said than done, and I simply couldn't do it.

Sure, I was accustomed to body shaming because of my size. I was accustomed to feeling bad about myself because of my weight—accustomed to feeling like a failure because I couldn't control it. Nonetheless, at that moment, I knew my life couldn't continue as it had in the past. I weighed over four hundred pounds; my knees creaked when I walked; and unless I was able to make some major changes, I was going to have to give up my beloved platform heels. But my issues were more than physical: I also wanted to be strong and positive for my children; I wanted to provide them with a healthy role model so they would have productive lives and make good choices. And emotionally, I definitely couldn't risk any more experiences like this one. I needed to lose weight, but just as important, I needed to improve my self-esteem. I couldn't afford to be devastated by negative events and judgments. My approach to life needed to change. I had to learn how to direct and control my emotions instead of allowing them to control me. I had to learn to rewrite my story, and I had to prove to myself that I could do it.

At My Heaviest

I weighed close to 425 pounds.

My hips measured as much as seventy-five inches around.

I couldn't always walk straight to get through a door; I had to turn sideways.

Even when I turned sideways I didn't always fit.

It was difficult for me to get in and out of even the roomiest vehicles.

Getting up and down stairs was a nightmare. Often I had to use my arms to move my leg up to the next stair. I would then hold on tight to the handrail to pull the rest of me up; this was a process I repeated for each stair.

If I walked more than a couple of blocks, I couldn't catch my breath and I would be drenched in sweat.

I loved dancing, but I could no longer do it.

My lower back and hips hurt all the time—often searing pain.

Getting on and off the couch was an aerobic exercise.

I wanted to go swimming, but I couldn't find a bathing suit that fit.

I tried improvising by wearing baggy shorts and a T-shirt. I was able to get into the pool, but when I tried to get out, the challenge was too great. My weight combined with the weight of the wet shorts meant that my bottom half was so heavy that it took a huge amount of effort to walk up the stairs to get out of the pool. It was a frightening experience because I didn't think I would make it.

I couldn't take normal trips with my children. If we went to Disneyland, for example, I always had to take a nanny. I didn't fit on any of the rides and didn't have the strength to stand in the long lines.

I couldn't even take a walk with my children.

If I saw a plus-size skirt I liked, I would sometimes buy two of the biggest size, which was a 28, and have a seamstress cut them and stitch them together to create one garment.

I was so big that many clothing companies wouldn't hire me—even for plus-size. My size didn't even exist in the mainstream—I had to make everything custom.

The Call

I was barely back from New York when my phone rang.

It was Alexandra Boos, a three-decade pioneer in the plus-size industry. She'd been a model herself (Alexandra is a curvy, sexy blonde with piercing blue eyes) and now is on the representation side of the business. I'd met Alexandra at Full Figured Fashion Week a few months back—she was on a panel called "Plus-Size Opportunity," and right away I noticed that she had great energy. After the panel, I made a beeline to introduce myself. Unlike so many of the businesspeople I spoke to that week, when we talked, she really looked me in the eye; I felt she really *saw* me. We'd chatted a few times since then, and I knew she was interested in me, but nothing had been finalized. Still, the more we talked, the more I saw her deeply spiritual side, and I was coming to know that she was trustworthy.

That call was a huge mix of emotions for me. Alexandra told me that she had been paying attention to my journey; she had seen the progress I'd made, but she also knew that I was not as successful as I wanted to be. She told me she applauded my desire to break the false barriers that kept larger women from seeing themselves as acceptable, let alone beautiful. My heart nearly broke in two when she told me that she could see the light in me and that she could tell I had a heart full of kindness and was someone who could make a powerful impact on the world. She asked me to tell her all my dreams. I poured out my soul to her.

And then she asked, "How bad do you want this, Rosie?"

Here's where the rubber hit the road. Alexandra explained to me that 67 percent of all women in America wear a size 14 or above—many, *way* above. The *average* dress size of an American woman is 16! But the plus-size designer samples used for photo shoots range from 14 to only 18, and typically on the lower side.

"It's not discrimination, Rosie," she said. "You aren't getting work because you don't fit the sample size."

In my mind, I flashed back to a particularly painful episode.

For one brief moment when I became a plus-size model, I thought that there would be less body shaming in my life. But I was very much mistaken. Something I quickly discovered is that models—plus-size or not—take it for granted that they will regularly be judged and, yes, shamed, often harshly, for each and every one of their so-called imperfections. I was a full-blown curvy girl with extremely large hips and a stomach that was far from flat. When I started modeling, I was an honest size 34—if you put a tape measure around my hips, it barely made it all the way around because my hips measured about six feet.

On one of my earliest jobs, I was called up for a shoot featuring a line of very pretty dresses designed for plus-size women. Within the first fifteen minutes, I realized that I was in the middle of a nightmare because I was expected to fit into a sample size 14. Impossible! It wasn't going to happen. But I was the only model there, and they were on deadline to finish the shoot.

"We don't have anybody else! We have to use her!" somebody said.

The only way they could make the dresses fit my body was by cutting them open in the back. So that's what they did, all the while complaining that my body was responsible for damaging the samples. All around me people were giggling. They thought the situation was hilarious. Even the woman wielding the scissors, the one who told me that I shouldn't expect the company to ever hire me again, was struggling not to laugh. I just had to stand there, trying to do my job. On the outside, I may have been smiling and trying to make the camera happy, but on the inside, all I wanted to do was cry. In the end, the company received such a positive response to the ads that they *did* ask me to model for them again, but at that moment, listening to the scissors cutting through fabric, I was humiliated and, yes, feeling guilty about the ruined outfits. I remember the thoughts going through my head: What made me think that I could be a successful model?

Then I flashed back to my painful humiliation at the airport. And to outings with my kids, when I didn't have the stamina to really *be* with them and had to hand off those moments of enjoyment to a nanny. I could feel tears gathering in my eyes.

I wanted a successful modeling career. I also wanted to be able to do some of the normal everyday things that I saw others doing. I dreamed of spontaneously going zip-lining, playing with my kids on a beach or a playground, getting on a bike, or taking a long hike in the woods. I kept dreaming, and I kept trying to lose weight. I must have tried every diet plan out there. I would lose weight—twenty pounds, thirty pounds, even fifty pounds or more, but I couldn't maintain. My weight yo-yoed all over the place. I thought of a *Curvy Girls* segment where I went to a gym, and the trainer asked, "What do you weigh?"

I answered, "Three fifteen." I wasn't trying to lie—315 was what I had weighed the last time I weighed myself.

He insisted I get on the scale. "Three forty."

I continued smiling for the camera, but I was totally humiliated.

Alexandra's question echoed in my mind: "How bad do you want this, Rosie?" And then she said, "I believe in you and your journey. I am a strong woman of faith, and I am getting a clear message that you have a big calling. I want to represent you and support you. I will try to get you work. I'm guessing at size twenty-eight you are close to four hundred pounds right now. Are you willing to get down to a size eighteen?"

I knew getting to a size 18 meant losing well over one hundred pounds. I took a deep breath and said with as much conviction as I could muster, "Yes. I am."

When it comes to trainers, Justin Blum of Las Vegas's Raw Fitness is the top of the top. He is an amazing miracle worker. We talked on the phone, and I told him the truth: "I'm a big girl who wants to lose weight."

"Get your ass over here."

Just looking at Justin, a vibrant and healthy-looking tall guy with an incredible well-toned physique, is inspiring. It's also fun. I especially appreciated that he wasn't judgmental and never said or did anything that made me feel bad about myself.

His approach was straightforward. "I don't give a sh*t that you are fat," he said. "I want to see what you can create for yourself. You are capable, and I'm going to push you—and push you hard. I'm going to tell you right now that there will be times when you will hate me."

I committed myself to being part of a group for a six-week challenge.

Justin created a new meal plan for me. As far as food was concerned, there would be no more last-minute choices, no more looking through the refrigerator or grabbing a piece of bread or a handful of cookies just because I was hungry and that was what immediately caught my eye. The first thing I had to do for my new plan was to prep and prepare three days' worth of food. I was going to be eating healthy, already prepped food, and I was going to be eating every three hours. When I looked at the amount of food in Justin's recommended plan, I knew that I wasn't going to feel hungry.

But more than anything else, Justin was about exercise.

"Mercado, jog!"

"Mercado, move!"

He stood behind me and made me move. He made me run; he made me jump; he made me move as fast as I could. When I started with him, I couldn't jump because my body couldn't handle the weight. He created a form of jumping jacks that could be done without my feet actually leaving the ground.

And then there was the instruction I would never forget.

"It's a burpee, Mercado. Let's go!"

For those who don't know, a burpee is a full-body exercise that's sometime called a squat thrust. Here's how you do it:

Start in a standing position.

Move into a squat position, placing your hands on the ground.

Kick your feet back so that you are in a plank position with your arms extended downward, from the shoulders.

Using a jump movement, bring your feet back into a squat position.

Stand up and start all over again.

And How Many Burpees Can You Do in a Minute?

I said, "I can't do this."

Justin said, "I'm telling you, you can."

I was positive I would never be able to do it.

Justin said, "You're not trying. Don't accept what people have told you about yourself and give up. You can do this. It may take you half an hour to do one burpee, but you *can* do it. Figure out your own way to get it done. It doesn't have to be my way. It can be your way. But figure it out."

When I started with Justin, it took me well over a minute to do just one. He wanted me to reach a point where I could do ten a minute.

I did what I had to do. I did the meal prep; I drank lots of water; I worked out six times a week. I was losing weight, and people started following me, first on Facebook and eventually on Instagram as well. I lost weight—and more weight. I was so proud. I felt as though my heart was bursting out of my chest. And I loved being part of Justin's group. It was like being a member of a family. When I completed the six weeks, everybody clapped.

A Strategy to Stay Committed

I first started posting about my determination to lose weight on Facebook because I wanted to stay committed. I figured the more people who knew what I was trying to do, the more determined I would be to not give up. I posted about my progress, and I posted videos of my workout. At the time, I probably had about one hundred thousand Facebook followers, at least some of whom were also trying to lose weight. Many of these people commented and posted back. They asked me about my recipes. They asked for suggestions on how to stay committed to a diet and exercise program. Some of them were very enthusiastic as well as involved.

My commitment to get healthier started to pay off. I began to lose real weight. Almost as soon as I lost close to one hundred pounds, I started to get more work.

Alexandra said, "Oh my God, you are doing this!"

"It's a lifestyle," Justin said. "This is going to be for the rest of your life. Stop looking at it as though it's work, and don't let it eat you up alive."

Discover What You Can Create for Yourself

You are the creator of your life. When my trainer, Justin Blum, told me that he wanted to see what I could create for myself, I heard him loud and clear. One of the things I've learned in life is that your thoughts and intentions manifest in what happens to you on a daily basis. Anything you say or think, you become. It all starts in your mind. In this way, we each become our own creations—walking examples of our own intentionality. If we want to create change and transformation in our own lives, we have to start by changing and transforming our thoughts and attitude. The change begins on the inside, with an inner transformation of the mind and soul, then in the body. Then life will mirror the change back to you in every area of your life. The power of intention combined with relentless action will accomplish what you never imagined you could do! I dare you to try this for the next week of your life and see how everything starts shifting.

All of us have an amazing amount of power over what happens to us. Positive change is possible for you, me, and everybody else because we are our own creators.

Ultimately we are the ones who have to do the work in our own lives. But sometimes, if we are very lucky, we will have someone push us into a corner where we have to choose and be accountable for our choice. I am so grateful that when I got the call from Alexandra, I recognized it for what it was—my moment of truth, to choose and commit. I remember that the panel she was on when I met her was called "Plus-Size Opportunity." And I think of the "O" in opportunity as a big brass ring to grab hold of. When I grabbed hold of that ring, I was completely determined to create something amazing with my life.

It's time to create something amazing with your own life. DON'T FORGET TO GRAB HOLD OF YOUR OWN BRASS RING!

And just as Justin said, "GET THAT ASS MOVING!"

CHAPTER 10

Walk Your Own Truth

I LOST ONE HUNDRED POUNDS, AND THEN I LET DOWN MY guard for a minute—just a minute. And then I started gaining it back.

Did it start with a piece of bread? A small helping of rice pudding? Coffee with cream? Stuck in an airport and buying some mac and cheese? A few days of being on the road for shoots, eating fast food, and not being able to work out? All I know is that the weight started to creep up again. I felt like I was a total disaster.

Even worse than looking in the mirror was looking at the interior of my head. My emotional response to gaining weight was severe and crippling. I hated myself. Hated myself! I had worked so hard, and then the minute I had a few normal meals, my weight started to go up. I was overwhelmed with depression. Why did I eat that French toast with a side of bacon? Why did I put cream in my coffee? Did that extra little box of raisins really make a difference? How could that happen? I saw other people eating candy bars, and they didn't weigh four hundred pounds. Why did I have such a sh*tty metabolism? Why did I throw away months and months of doing burpees for a friggin' piece of pizza? Why did I self-sabotage? I felt like a depressed failure and, I repeat, I hated myself.

A Message

It was a Sunday morning. I had just come home from an assignment, and I was feeling totally disconsolate and depressed. I wanted to give up. I was so ashamed that I had regained some weight that I didn't want anybody to see me. The rest of my family went to church. I went back to bed and turned on the television and started watching an interview on Univision. Turning on this particular show at this particular time was one of those totally synchronistic, heaven-sent moments. An extremely famous Latina journalist, María Antonieta Collins, was being interviewed. And she was talking about her own struggles with weight and how beaten down she had been by being unable to lose it. María Antonieta is always an inspirational woman. But that day it felt as though she was talking to me personally, and as I watched, it was like an angel bringing me a personal message. As I listened to her, I completely identified. But the woman I was watching on TV was not overweight. She had found a solution to her issues with weight. How had she done it?

I was riveted as she described how she was tired of always feeling bad about herself because of her weight. Yes, that's how I felt too. She wanted to feel good about herself. That's exactly how I felt. Her solution to her issues with weight was bariatric surgery. As I listened to her speak, I thought, Why not? Maybe that could work for me.

The Research Begins

Monday morning I started to get information about doctors who did bariatric surgery, and I immediately zeroed in on Dr. Bernie Hanna, a surgeon in Las Vegas who seemed extremely qualified. I attended a seminar to learn more, and I made an appointment. I didn't tell anybody what I was doing. Nobody.

I knew I would need money to have the surgery. I still owned the house I bought when I was with Gianni. It was rented out short-term. But why not put it on the market? This was a major step, but I did it. It sold in less than a month.

When I went in to see Dr. Hanna, I asked, "How soon can I do this? What's the quickest way?"

He started to tell me that it could take months and months to get approval for my insurance. "No," I interrupted him. "I want to do it now."

"If you want to pay cash, we can do it tomorrow," he said, "but you don't want to pay cash."

"Yes, I do."

At first I don't think he believed me, but I convinced him that I was serious.

Well, it turned out that there were still several medical tests, which slowed down the process. Dr. Hanna also wanted me first to lose at least twenty pounds, and he wanted me to go on a liquid fast for a week. I think, among other things, he was trying to make sure that I was sufficiently motivated to do what I would have to do.

The liquid fast was hell. I was surrounded by food—pizza, Mexican bread, tortillas—and I couldn't have any of it. Fasting was a new experience. All I could think about was all the delicious food I wasn't eating. Unable to eat, I became obsessed with food. It felt as though the ice cream in the freezer was crying out to me. Temptation was everywhere, and I couldn't even have coffee. I had to go to Dr. Hanna's office every three days to be weighed and to be sure that I was properly hydrated. Finally, I got the go-ahead.

But I had another hurdle to cross: I still had to tell my family what I was planning to do. Two days before the surgery was scheduled, I told my mom that I was going into the hospital for an operation.

"My God! Are you sick? What's wrong?" she asked.

She didn't immediately understand that I was talking about bariatric surgery, but once she did, she was far from happy.

"Who is making fun of you?" she wanted to know. I could see the protective-mom look pass over her face—she was ready to go out and do battle with anyone who was making me unhappy.

"This is not about anybody else," I told her. "This is about me."

"Why?" she asked me. "Why are you so fascinated with being thin?"

"Mom," I told her, "I don't want to live like this for the rest of my life. And it's not about being thin. It's about not being as big as I am. I'm tired, Mom. Really tired."

"You are making a huge mistake," she argued.

If anything, my father was even less enthusiastic than my mom.

"You are risking your life," he said. "I don't think this is the right decision."

My brother was more succinct. "You've done some crazy sh*t in your life," he reminded me, "but this is the craziest."

Despite his concerns, my terrific brother signed on to be there with my mom when I woke up after surgery.

The Journey Begins for Real

Amazingly, I was only a little nervous when I showed up at the hospital at 5:00 A.M. I couldn't even imagine what was going to happen next. After the prep was finished, I was wheeled into the operating room and told to count back from ten. I think I got as far as nine.

The next thing I knew, I was waking up groggy and not even sure the surgery had happened. I felt no pain. When I looked at my stomach, I saw a small incision. I was hugging the cute little bear they gave me and wearing a pair of those big old ugly, ugly gray hospital socks.

"You are definitely the craziest one in this family," my brother said as he helped me stand, "but you did it." He supported me as I started walking a few steps as required.

Recovery was an amazing experience. When I had two sips of water, I felt absolutely full. When I told this to Dr. Hanna, he said, "Welcome to the world of bariatric surgery."

I don't think I had ever before in my life felt full. All my life, I would consume huge amounts of food, eating and eating and still feeling hungry. This was the first time in my life that I felt full.

I'll always remember coming home from the hospital and walking toward the house. My kids were waiting for me, and I could tell from the expressions on their faces that they didn't understand exactly what had happened. In the meantime, I was wondering if I was going to make it to the door and wanted to be sure that I didn't scare them by falling down.

What was I able to eat? Next to nothing! I was on a liquid diet for a week—water and protein shakes like Bariatric Advantage. Then I graduated to pureed food. For at least a month I was existing on small quantities of pureed food. I actually started to like soft, mushed-up food—in small quantities. I would puree a carrot, eat three or four small teaspoons, and announce that I was done with my meal. Almost like a baby progressing from liquids to pureed foods then to foods that are progressively thicker, I had to learn to eat again. I quickly realized that if I tried eating too many carbs or sugar, I'd start to get a little dizzy. My body kept warning me not to overeat or eat the wrong foods.

Building a Different Relationship with Food

It goes without saying that food always had a special place in my heart—*especialmente la comida Mexicana.* I loved everything about food—breakfast, lunch, dinner, snacks. At the moment when I was actually eating, I was always happy. Of course, after I had crammed every last crumb on the table down my throat, I felt guilty and stupid and like a total failure.

I was a classic emotional eater. I didn't just eat because I felt hungry. I ate as a response to any one of a dozen common emotions. Whenever I was stressed, angry, or frustrated, I headed for the refrigerator. I also ate when I was lonely, and I especially ate when I was bored. Food was my readily available go-to way of soothing my feelings—almost a form of self-medication. Even when I was happy and things were going well—that's also when I rewarded myself with food. And the kind of food I craved the most? All kinds of comfort food—anything that was filled with carbohydrates and grease topping the list. If I was emotional about anything in my life, I responded by stuffing myself.

After surgery, I had to develop some new and better patterns. The surgery reduced the amount of food I was even *able* to eat. This changed not only my eating habits but my social habits. Although I had certainly been a solitary eater—and sometimes even a middle-of-the-night eater, I also used food as a way of connecting with the people around me—particularly my family. When we sat down to eat together, we also communicated, sharing the stuff that was going on with our lives.

My bariatric surgery impacted how I related not only to food but also to others around food. This was a major adjustment. When I ate dinner, slowly and carefully chewing my small portions, at first my family looked at me as though I was some kind of alien being, in danger of starving herself to death. One would ask, "That's all you are going to eat? You're really *done*?" Another might chime in, "You need to eat more or you are going to get sick!"

Remember that I come from a family of large people, and all of us enjoyed eating. That was the norm. Before the surgery, I fit right in. After surgery, I would be eating a small portion of salad and chicken while they were chowing down on rice, beans, chicken, chips, tamales, pizza, pasta, salad, and dessert. Hot damn, they ate a lot. I would stare at the massive amounts of food they were consuming and realize that for most of my life, I had been doing the same thing.

My new relationship with food changed my attitude toward a lot of things I previously enjoyed. Take going to restaurants, for example. Although it was great to go into a restaurant and not worry about whether I was going to break the chair by sitting on it, ordering carefully and eating only small portions from the appetizer menu definitely changed the experience. Eating in restaurants made me self-conscious, and dessert became much less important to me. It seemed as though there was no purpose to eating out and, when I did so, I usually felt like a stranger in a strange land.

After the surgery, people looked at me differently. I'd become accustomed to people staring at my hips in wonderment and awe, as though I was on display. It was horrible, and I couldn't get over my discomfort and unhappiness when that happened, which was pretty much always. After surgery, as I started to lose more and more weight, I started to be more confident about how I carried myself. Nobody was smirking or laughing at my hips. People were now staring at my face and looking into my eyes.

The very best thing that happened is that my relationship with my kids changed. I was actually able to do things with them. I was able to take a walk with them, and when I did, I wasn't crazy out of breath, perspiring and flushed. I had more energy than ever before. We could go places together. I could actually get up and play with them.

Many everyday activities became easier. Getting in and out of the car, for example, was no longer an aerobic workout. Neither was getting on and off a toilet. I didn't have to waste time worrying about the simplest things. We could, for example, make a plan to go to a movie without my being nervous about whether I would fit into the seat or be able to use the public bathroom. For the very first time I could go on outings with the kids without taking a nanny because for the first time I was able to keep up. I could even go on the rides at Disneyland. For each moment of my life, there was simply more happiness and less pain.

And, for the first time in years, I was able to dance my way through an entire song, having fun and enjoying it. I started taking Latin dance classes; my losing weight also increased the movement in my kids' lives because we went together as a family to Zumba class. And I loved it!!!!

My only brother, the one who told me that my getting bariatric surgery made me the craziest family member, was the first to fold. He told me, "I want to have the energy you have—I want to be able to run after my sons." In less than a year, he signed up for surgery and, like me, ultimately lost two hundred pounds. Now, I love watching him move and be happy.

Soon after, my sister Priscilla signed up for surgery. She was followed by my mother, my sister Lily, and, finally, my dad. Seeing what I was now able to do and the way my life had been transformed by surgery inspired them to do the same. They all had successful results. Now, we still eat together, but we are on the same page about portions and healthy eating. When we sit down to eat as a family, we are probably all eating reasonable-size portions, but we are still enjoying wonderful coffee, and we are still having fun.

It was all good except for one thing: I was losing weight so rapidly that my social media followers couldn't help but notice that something dramatic was going on with my body. I probably should have posted something and clued them in when I made the decision to have bariatric surgery. But remember, I hadn't even told my family until two days before I entered the hospital. It's not that I forgot about my followers; it's just that I was totally focused on keeping up my courage and maintaining my commitment to follow through with my decision.

And something else had made me hesitate. In the days immediately following my surgery, I called various advisors and agents to share what I had just done. They were more than ambivalent about my posting and going public on social media. They warned me about backlash, saying things like, "Don't do it! You will ruin your career!"

Alexandra Boos, my manager, was the only one who gave me different advice. She reminded me of the importance of remaining authentic and honest. She said, "Truth always wins—you always have to speak from a place of truth, no matter what the consequences." Alexandra had been my rock, and I trusted her completely.

Like Alexandra, I pride myself on being honest and knew I couldn't keep it all a secret, nor did I really want to. I never made a formal announcement, per se, but soon I began sharing details about my bariatric surgery and recovery process. Despite the problems involved with recovery, a limited diet, and becoming accustomed to a new way of eating, I was feeling extremely happy about having the surgery. One of the best results, of course, was that I could finally fit into a plus-size sample 14 or 16, which meant that I started to get more work. More work meant that the likelihood of my being able to support my children increased. But many on social media were less than enthusiastic.

Why Am I Getting Hate Mail?

Even before my first post about my recovery, I started to get hate mail from fat activists as well as men and women—now former social media followers—who correctly guessed that I'd had bariatric surgery and were extremely angry at me for doing so. I must admit that I was shocked by the anger. I had been determined to lose weight because I wanted to be able to hang out and do things with my children. I wanted to get rid of the pain in my hips and knees, and I wanted to be healthy. Now I was being bashed for my efforts. *Por qué las criticas, Rosie?*

By talking about my journey and posting "before" and "after" photos, some fat activists said that I was guilty of fat shaming other plus-size women. I was reminded again and again that some people take the body positivity movement to the extreme—going so far as to suggest that really heavy men and women, just like I was at 420 pounds, should be so happy and positive about their weight that they should never want to lose any of it. The truth is that whether you lose weight, gain weight, or stay the same, you should never be shamed for your decision. Your life and the decisions you make for it are your own personal choice. You have to define your own happiness.

Certainly, when I lost weight, I received a great deal of support, but I also received more than a few over-the-top negative reactions. Mail came from people who accused me of having Hollywood beauty standards, saying things like, "You look just like a plastic Barbie!" "Sellout" was a common accusation. Others insulted me for "taking the easy way out." Some plus-size women expressed feelings of genuine betrayal. They said things like, "You must have been ashamed of your body all along!" One man wrote to tell me that I was no longer beautiful. I was especially confused and hurt by a famous plus-size model and fat activist who quickly labeled me both a liar and a sellout. She told her followers that they shouldn't support someone like me. She implied that she thought my message was telling people that being fat meant that you were also unhappy.

The strongest response I received came from a woman who told me that she used to admire me, but now she hated me. "Why," she asked, "don't you just jump off a bridge and kill yourself?!" I still remember my shock when I read this message. What the . . . ? It was such an extreme reaction, and I couldn't help feeling pained.

During this same time period, I had to go to Los Angeles, and at the airport, a *TMZ* reporter spotted me standing at the baggage claim and started asking questions about my weight loss and people's reactions. He asked if I missed anything about the weight, and I basically told him no but that I was grateful for having had the experience of weighing as much as I had because I had learned a great deal. When he asked what, I answered him by saying, "Humble, how to treat people, never judge a book by its cover, and persistence." The story ran on *TMZ* with the headline, "I Lost 240 Pounds . . . and People Said 'Kill Yourself.'"

Once Again, My Story Goes Viral

The *TMZ* interview, which went viral, changed everything in my career path. I've honestly lost track of all the people who wanted to interview me to talk about my surgery and the aftermath. A large number of major magazines like *People* and *Cosmopolitan* as well as newspapers in both the US and Europe published stories. I was amazed by the amount of attention my story received. Television shows like *Dr. Phil* and *The Doctors* did segments, and there was a story on Univision.

But I still faced some negative reactions. Some people on social media continued to accuse me of such things as being addicted to plastic surgery, saying that I had also had a facelift and a nose job. Not true, but people insisted on repeating incorrect information. The false plastic surgery stories made me feel like, "Damn, do I really look fake?" I couldn't understand. Why were so many people looking so hard to find fault with me? For sure, those responses were upsetting, and I had to really work to not let them get to me.

I felt as though I needed to do something. My good friend, photographer Jerry Metellus, helped me pull my thoughts together and get up the courage to speak up, I finally ended up posting a short video of my own in response to the haters, including the person who told me to jump off a bridge and die. Doing this gave me a sense of empowerment.

The little video I posted was titled "To the Hater Who Told Me to Kill Myself after Losing 250 Pounds." Here's what I said . . .

For those of you that don't know me, my name is Rosie Mercado. And I am a mother, a daughter, a friend, a lover of life. I recently lost 250 pounds and have received an overwhelming response of love, support—just kind words from around the world, and I'm grateful for that. But with the positive comes a little bit of negative, and I want to take the time to acknowledge a message that really stood out and made me think. This message was sent directly to me, and the message was: "Go find a bridge, jump off, and kill yourself." The message was to go find a bridge to jump off and kill myself because I had lost weight. This message got me thinking so much that I wanted to thank you and I wanted to take the time to invite you to come join me at a beautiful bridge, because I love bridges. And I want to invite you to come see it from my perspective, because the view from here is beautiful. It's amazing! But if you choose to stay down there and expect a splash, just know that the only thing you will see is a shadow of me jumping and taking flight, because the only way I'm going is up. I'm thankful for everything in my life. And this is something that I'm thankful for, because I appreciate my life and the beauty it has within it. So with that said, thank you. I'm taking flight. And the only way is up.

Making and posting this video was a very important step for me to take for my psychological health and well-being. I think when I received negative feedback about my weight loss it reminded me of all the times when I was bullied and didn't stand up for myself. A life lesson I've learned many times over is that it is always important for us to stand firm and not retreat from the world. I very much needed to speak up for who I was and what I believed.

We live in a strange world in which bullies can hide behind their computers, tablets, and phones and post anything they want to say on social media, no matter how horrible or hateful. It was important for me to issue a statement that made my opinion clear: There is too much hate in the world, and I didn't want to add to it.

A Practical Problem

Okay, I lost the weight, and my body was transformed, but when I looked at myself in the mirror without clothes on, I was less than thrilled. I must have been really out of touch not to realize that I would have to do something about all the loose skin. I looked horrible. There were pounds and pounds of skin. I didn't want people looking at me to immediately be aware of the folds of skin hanging all over my body. It created serious difficulties for someone trying to make a living as a model—even as a plus-size model. Before I got dressed and walked out the door to go someplace, I had to put on Spanx to squish my loose skin together. But Spanx also created different problems in the form of rashes and itchy spots where moisture would hide out. I was grateful that I had lost weight, but there was no getting around my new problem. My message has always been to love your body, no matter how you look. But faced with the reality of so much hanging skin, it was sometimes hard for me to hold on to that thought. Once I started getting rashes, I was grossed out by my itchy body. Hanging skin can also create unpleasant smells. To avoid this, it felt as though I spent much of my day in the shower.

About a year and a half after my bariatric surgery, I had another surgery—this one for skin removal. This time I went to Mexico—to Dr. Carlos Buenrostro, another guardian angel doctor, who warned me up front that this was not an easy procedure. When I had my initial appointment with him, he told me two things that resonated. One, it was going to be painful, and, two, to relax because I was in good hands. Both were true.

I wasn't accustomed to showing anyone my naked body, and I honestly worried that my first examination would make me incredibly uncomfortable. I always appreciate anyone who is not judgmental. Dr. Buenrostro, a very kind person, was able to examine me without making me feel bad about how I looked in any way. As he listened to me describe all my problems, he was reassuring as well as professional. He explained that this would not be an overnight process. It would take time, effort, and work, but we would get through it together.

On the day of the surgery, I arrived at the hospital early in the morning without any makeup, and one of the first things they did was use a marker to outline parts of my body—hip to hip. I was in surgery for six hours, and there was too much loose skin for them to address all of it. There was only so much they could do, but they were able to complete a tummy tuck. By the time they were finished, they had removed more than twenty pounds of skin. Looking at my body after surgery, Dr. Buenrostro seemed genuinely enthusiastic and as excited about my transformation as I was.

When I woke up, I was in so much pain that I couldn't talk. Even breathing was painful. If I had to cough, the pain was excruciating. They told me that I had to stand up and walk to avoid blood clots. I still remember trying to stand and discovering that I had absolutely no upper body strength. When I looked down, I could see my ugly hospital socks, and then everything went gray and I passed out. I heard someone yelling, "Grab her!" as I went down.

A couple of days later, when I was finally able to stand and look down, I was shocked. For the first time in my life, I could see my pubic area. I couldn't laugh because of the pain in my stomach muscles, but I wanted to. "Guess what?" I said to my doctor. "I can see my vagina!"

He laughed.

I'm Still Plus-Size

Now that it is all said and done, I do look smaller than I did when my journey started, but I'm still a curvy Latina woman with large hips. Some people who heard about my weight loss automatically assumed that I was trying to get "skinny" using an "easy" way out. That wasn't my goal: I was trying to get healthy. Trust me, everything I did was not an "easy way." It was hard and scary and felt as though I was putting my life on the line. But I wanted to stop worrying about whether my children were going to be left without a mother—or whether my kids would be stuck with a mother who was so heavy that they would end up having to take care of her, perhaps even having to lift her in and out of bed. That was a terrifying thought.

The gastric sleeve operation was a great tool to start my weight loss, but it's still been a long journey full of dedication and hard work. There has been nothing easy about the process. I still need to eat carefully and exercise strenuously to make sure that I don't regain pounds. I'm often in the gym. The good part is that I am now able to do this. At my heaviest, it was almost impossible for me to do many of the exercises. At four hundred pounds, for example, it was almost impossible for me to do any jumping. Now, when my work schedule means that I don't have time to get to the gym, I have a trainer who comes to the house and works out with me—and often with my kids as well.

Watching My Weight

I will always have a tendency to put on weight, and I will never have the kind of metabolism that allows me to eat anything I want. I will always have to work out. Currently, four days a week I do a boot camp–type workout with weight lifting and interval training. I mix it up with Zumba, Zumba, Zumba, which I love and was unable to do when I was at my heaviest.

If I'm stressed or if something is going wrong in my life, I have to remind myself of my issues with emotional eating. I'm very careful not to make the refrigerator my go-to first choice for instant comfort. When I first went on various television shows, for example, I was a little nervous about my new role. I wanted to do a good job, and I wanted to be able to help people. There are always snacks like chips and salsa backstage, and I had to be careful not to abuse them. Once again, my anxieties led me straight to food. When I did this, I quickly gained a few pounds. It was a reminder that I could never turn my back on all the work I'd done to reach my current weight.

Emotional eating is a struggle for many of us. Not only do we eat when we are sad or unhappy, we also eat when we feel celebratory. I know people—I guess we all do—who seem to be capable of eating huge amounts of all kinds of food, everything from candy bars to soda, without gaining an ounce. I'm not one of them, and I will never be one of them. A fact of my life is that I can never again fall back on addictive eating to soothe my psyche.

Who I Am and What I Learned

Body shaming takes many forms. When I was 420 pounds, I was regularly body shamed by people who called me mean, ugly names for being too fat. When I had surgery and lost weight, I was called a different group of mean, ugly names. It felt as though I would never be good enough and there would always be people who wanted to talk sh*t. I learned that there are men and women who are always waiting to find fault. I've learned that this is a reflection of how these people feel about themselves. Unless they are able to change their outlook, happiness may well elude them. I absolutely know that I cannot make their story my story.

My body will never be perfect. Although my waist is small, my hips and butt are still very large. My thighs are also thick, and I wear a small bra size. In short, I'm very disproportionate, and, I still have cellulite. Because of my body type, there are people who will always look at me and call me fat. But it's my body, and I'm happy to be able to walk and dance and work out. Accepting and loving my body has been a learning process and experience. When I was at my heaviest and regularly eating everything in sight as well as accepting sh*tty relationships, I now realize that I was punishing myself. I was my own worst bully. I used to try to go on crash diets hoping to reach a specific number or weight. I now know that what matters is not my weight. That's just a number. What matters is my mental well-being and how I feel about myself. That's what really counts.

I affirm: I am a true beauty, perfectly imperfect.

Walk Your Own Truth

We are each different. We are each unique. Each one of us is an example of God's creation. We should never define ourselves—or anybody else—by the number of pounds we carry around with us or, for that matter, the clothes we put on. Our thoughts, feelings, emotions, and goals are more essential to who we are than what we see when we step on a scale or look in a mirror. What's truly important in this life is authenticity and learning to walk in our own truth.

Wayne Dyer said it best, so I'm just going to quote him:

> *The essential lesson I've learned in life is to just be yourself. Treasure the magnificent being that you are and recognize first and foremost you're not here as a human being only. You're a spiritual being having a human experience.*

In my life, I had to hold tight to my own authentic spirit and learn not to pay attention to criticism or name-calling. I am who I am. And so are you! There is NO mistake in who you are.

CHAPTER 11

Notice and Respond from the Heart

I WAS RAISED CATHOLIC AND LEARNED STRUCTURED PRAYERS, like the Lord's Prayer, but as I got older, I started attending different churches and began to expand my idea of what it means to pray and talk to God. I started to actively incorporate prayer into my daily life and began to see it more as an ongoing conversation with the Divine Presence, who can hear and is aware of everything that we say, do, and think.

After each of my relationships fell apart and when I became ill, many of my prayers were of the "God, how could you let this happen to me?" and "Why are you not helping?" variety. Then, as both my attitude and health began to improve, I started realizing all the ways in which God had been helping. Doors had consistently been opening for me: I had found doctors and treatments; I had found information as well as inspiration. I started to see that God and the Divine appeared to aid me in a zillion ways. I'm reminded of the old joke about the man who lived in a waterside town that suffered a large storm and floods. He climbed to his roof and waited for God to come save him. The fire department showed up to help, people in boats of various sizes arrived, even a helicopter appeared. To all of them the man said, "It's okay. I'm waiting for God to come rescue me." The man was finally swept into the waters and after he died and arrived at the pearly gates, he confronted God. "What happened?" he asked. "I prayed and waited for you to save me."

"What happened?" replied God, who was incredulous at the man's stupidity. "I sent the fire department; I sent all those boats; I even sent a helicopter. Why didn't you grab on to something?"

In my own life, I know that I've been sent a great deal of help, and I like to think that I've been able grab on to the help that's been offered.

Leaning into My Faith

We are all on spiritual journeys, walking paths that ideally will help us learn more about ourselves, our faith, and the spiritual connections that tie us to one another, the universe, and God. I am grateful that I was born into a family of faith. Growing up, I always knew that my parents were up before dawn praying together for the well-being of the family. It's a wonderful feeling to know that your mom and dad are there, praying for you every single day. I was profoundly aware of my Mexican *abuelita*'s (my mom's mom) relationship with God because it permeated and was part of everything she said and did, but she didn't insist that her grandchildren, or anyone else, share her belief system. Completely accepting and nonjudgmental, she was all about faith and prayer. I always thought of her as being spiritually perfect.

Anyone visiting my California *abuelita* (my dad's mom) was also aware of her faith by her words as well as the large number of saint candles that dotted her home. She was far from traditional in her spiritual practices, but she was a believer who always did what resonated with her personal vibration. Always a free spirit, my California grandmother was open to new ways of including spirituality in her life. She showed me how to use incense and put oil in candles and told me, "You have to do whatever makes you feel energized, centered, and connected." This grandmother also taught me how to sage my house and how to lift my prayerful petitions to a higher presence.

Neither my parents nor my grandparents ever preached about their beliefs or forced me to follow their example. I did attend Catholic school, run by a priest whose outward approach to life seemed far removed from Christian teachings about love and patience, and I always felt as though the school itself did little to increase my relationship with God. However, enough of my parents' and *abuelitas*' strong faith must have seeped into my being that when I was troubled about something, almost as a reflexive motion, I would often utter a prayer, asking for help and guidance. When my daughter's father left me, for example, I remember falling to my knees pleading with God to do something—anything—to relieve my intense pain and anxiety.

My realization that I wanted a deeper and more meaningful connection to God began when I was struggling to recover from that brain cyst you heard about in chapter 1. That's when I began to reflect on the power of faith and pray on a daily basis for help, healing, and guidance. I realized I wanted to incorporate my faith into my daily life.

When we ask for God's aid, I truly believe that HE sends us people and situations that help us move in the directions we are meant to go. All we have to do is notice that they are there and respond from the heart. One of the people who has been most instrumental in helping me maintain a spiritual path is my manager, Alexandra Boos, who has what she refers to as a prayer-based business model, which means that she tries to integrate prayer and faith into all her work.

Soon after we met, Alexandra and I became prayer partners. When we first started doing this, I was on my weight loss journey, and that was the focus of many of my personal prayers. Now, we try to pray together on a daily basis about all the areas of both of our lives. We are both committed to doing this. Before making any decisions, I pray about it alone, as well as with Alexandra. I pray that God will guide me and show me what I am meant to do and where I am meant to be. I pray for clarity, discernment, and awareness and ask that God will use me and my life to help others. If I need help in a particular area of my life, I write it down and ask that God helps me reach answers, opens up doors, and gives me signs that I am doing what I am supposed to do. Faith is an essential part of my life, and one of my favorite maxims is "Faith moves mountains. Doubt creates them."

Whatever I do, I ask for God's involvement and guidance. A favorite Bible passage from Matthew 7:7–8 (ESV) that I read and repeat often is:

> *Ask, and it will be given to you; seek, and you will find; knock, and it will be opened to you. For everyone who asks receives, and the one who seeks finds, and to the one who knocks it will be opened.*

I truly believe that if we turn to God in faith, we will find answers, solutions, and sometimes even miraculous results.

Through prayer, I have become better able to surrender my life to God. "Jesus take the wheel!" I used to suffer from anxiety and panic attacks. But surrendering my problems to God has really helped me get rid of much of my anxiety. I trust that God will help me get through whatever occurs. He has showed up in my life in so many beautiful ways. I can't physically see Him, but I feel His presence. I find this approach significantly more effective than taking addictive medication for anxiety. Everyone is different, but this is what works for me.

Developing a stronger relationship with God has also helped me understand that there is a deeper purpose in all of our challenges and problems—pretty much everything we go through. Leaning into my faith can be a challenge, but doing so has helped me trust a Higher Power. I believe there is always a reason for all of our struggles. Every *no* we receive in life is a test. Firming up this belief has taught me how to surrender, let go, and trust God. This is not always easy for me. I tend to be a stubborn person who wants what I want when I want it. But sometimes when you are not getting answers or results, the only thing you can do is wait patiently. I have found that when you become extremely pushy to the point of desperation, there is a good chance that you will push away what you want. But when you gracefully knock on the door and let the universe know that you are ready, you attract opportunities in your life and are better able to manifest your dreams. The key is to have faith and surrender. In the right time, you will have what is yours.

There is a purpose to my life—to all our lives. So long as I am still breathing, there is something I am supposed to be doing here on this earth. This is the path I want to walk. In recent years, my children and I started going to church on a regular basis. Doing this gives me a sense of peace, spiritual connection, and growth. I want Bella, Valentino, Alex, and Emiliano to have a strong faith that sustains them when they face challenges in their own lives.

Having said that, I also believe that we always need to do everything we can on a practical level, based on inspiration, to help us move forward in the direction we are meant to go. You can't look at a sink full of dirty dishes and expect it to disappear. As much as you may pray for favor and grace from God, you still have to pour on the soap and roll up your sleeves.

Learning to Meditate: A Predetermined Accident

As my belief and sense of spiritual connectedness have grown, I've become more aware of other ways of strengthening my spiritual core. Although I'm convinced that there are no accidents in life, my introduction to meditation came about through what can best be described as a predetermined accident. I was by myself, driving around Vegas, when the symbols on a Buddhist temple caught my attention. When I'm driving anywhere, I'm usually in a hurry—rushing to pick up the kids or get back home. But on this day, I had some extra time, so when I noticed the temple, I parked the car and got out for a closer look. On the side of the building I saw an Asian man—a monk—probably in his fifties, with beads on his wrist and wearing a saffron robe. He was gardening. I summoned my courage to approach a stranger and walked up to him.

"Can I help you?" he asked. I immediately noticed that he seemed very kind and friendly, as well as peaceful.

"Yes," I replied. "I am interested in finding out what you teach here."

He suggested we go into the temple, and I felt completely comfortable doing that. Once inside, he asked, "Have you ever meditated or chanted?"

"No."

"Would you like to learn?"

I nodded, and he began to talk to me about the importance of "being present" for life.

I wasn't exactly sure what he meant by "being present." He quietly explained about meditation and learning to savor the present moment.

"Let's breathe," he said as he began to guide me through my first meditation.

Sitting with this kind monk, I also received a brief lesson in chanting. This was very much a "say yes" moment in my life. The mantra he taught me is a Green Tara Mantra. The monk told me that this mantra helps the chanter overcome physical, emotional, mental, and relationship blocks. The Green Tara figure is called upon to offer assistance. The only requirement is for the chanter not to cling to any one outcome; the more detached and non-grasping we can be, the happier the outcome. Here's the mantra:

OM TARE TUTTARE TURE SOHA OM

I invoke the Universal sound Tare: And the Green Tara
Tuttare: To bring deliverance from suffering and delusion
Ture: Paving the way for compassion and Enlightenment
Soha: I offer this prayer to Green Tara.

This was my first chant. As the monk explained the chant, I wondered how he knew what my heart needed. Listening to him speak, I absolutely felt guided. When I left the temple, I felt lighter, as though I had released some of the burdens weighing on me. I was excited to learn more about meditation, and I was also interested in finding out whether other religious traditions might help me find answers for my life. I had so many questions. Why did I continue to overeat even though I was gaining weight? Why had my romantic relationships failed? Was I choosing the wrong men, and why were they attracted to me? Why was I so often anxious, and what could I do about it?

Interestingly, however, I never went back to the temple. For one thing, between my work and caring for my children, I didn't really have the time. For another, I was not Buddhist, and my visit at the temple was a small private journey. I was born Roman Catholic and, as silly as it sounds, at the time, I also honestly wondered if my hanging out at a Buddhist temple might somehow offend God. As I've grown spiritually, I've realized that meditation, which helped ground me, fit in with the whole picture. I walked away from my encounter with the peaceful monk thinking that if meditation could help me calm down, then I was all for doing it. From that day forward, every morning I began to include a ten-minute meditation as a way to start my day.

Nurturing My Spirit in Less Traditional Ways

When I decided to take my first seminar with Tony Robbins, I don't know what I hoped to accomplish. I was walking into the unknown unlocking a new door, hoping to have something new and better than what I had before. I had been reading people like Deepak Chopra, Wayne Dyer, and Iyanla Vanzant for years, and they had been extraordinarily important in helping me find a more spiritual and meaningful path. But I had mostly avoided Tony Robbins. This was an obvious act of rebellion against my dad, who had been telling me about Tony Robbins for so many years that the mere mention of his name had become annoying. For as long as I could remember, Dad had been pushing me to read Tony Robbins's books and listen to his tapes. Dad, who strongly believed that Tony Robbins knew more about living a successful life than anyone else, also kept asking me to attend a seminar. I was more than a little skeptical as well as reluctant, but, dragging my feet, I went off to attend a seminar called "Unleash the Power Within," primarily to please my father. It was held at the Los Angeles Convention Center, and my daughter, who was eleven at the time, came with me.

I expected to be bored as well as annoyed by Robbins. But that's not what happened. It was an amazing four-day event. I laughed, I cried, I danced, and I walked on burning coals. My daughter was right there with me. Our days started early in the morning and sometimes went on until 2:00 A.M. There were so many people with so many different reasons for being there. I think all the participants wanted to create some form of serious and enduring change in their lives. We all had barriers we wanted to overcome; we all had goals we wanted to achieve. People were focused on everything from getting healthy and losing weight to improving relationships, finding jobs, starting businesses, and making more money. In my case, I also think sharing this time with my daughter provided a real bonding experience.

People often describe peak experiences as being life-changing. This truly was. I came away with so much more passion as well as greater clarity about who I was and where I wanted to go. The event gave me a better picture of my goals as well as a plan about how to get there. It taught me that it isn't enough to just show up—you have to show up with a message—and, like Tony Robbins says, "Take massive action."

Setting Powerful Goals: How the Teachings of Tony Robbins Changed My Life

Recently there has been some negative press about Robbins, accusing him of inappropriate behavior and worse. I never experienced any of this alleged behavior personally, nor did I witness any. That does not mean that I, in any way, want to diminish the experiences of people who have different memories. In my case, Robbins's teachings added so much value to my life, and I am grateful that at that time in my life, I was able to experience that growth. In terms of pure motivation, he has to be the single most inspiring speaker ever. Later, after my initial experiences with Tony, I would also attend Robbins University.

I came away from the "Unleash the Power Within" seminar with a whole new view of what I wanted to achieve in life. But the seminar did more than offer inspiration; it provided some powerful practical tools to help me define my goals as well as what I had to do to achieve them. Focus has always been an issue in my life—I have a tendency to jump from thing to thing without zeroing in on where I want to be and what I want to do. Robbins stressed the importance of being clear about what we want to achieve. This was an important message for me to hear.

A question we all need to ask ourselves: How can I reach my goals if I'm not even sure what they are?

It helps if we can actually *see* our goals in some concrete way. So for me, one of the most effective tools that Robbins suggested involved creating a vision board—a collage of assorted images as well as possible lines of text that represent what is important to you or what you hope to achieve. Having these pictures and words in front of you keeps your intentions fresh and clear in your mind, so that you constantly direct your energy and actions toward accomplishing them.

Almost as soon as I got home, I started to create a vision board for myself. Tony Robbins is not the only motivational thinker and influencer to suggest that each of us will benefit from having our own unique vision, but he is the one whose words and energy inspired me to act.

A Personal Vision Board

Creating your very own vision board for the goals you want to achieve or the life you want to manifest is one of the first steps you can take, as well as one of the easiest things you can do. It's also one of the most powerful. My vision board helps me stay determined as well as focused. Many people create vision boards by using large poster boards, corkboards, or any other kind of presentation board. If you look online, you will find dozens of tips and hints about what to use and how to put your board together. More important than the physical act of gathering the necessary material to make the board is what you decide to put on it. When you construct a vision board, you want it to represent the life you want to lead—providing daily reminders of exactly where you want to be.

I was very careful about putting together a vision board that represented what I wanted my life to look like—and what I wanted to see around me. When you create a vision board, it's important that you be able to look at the images on your board and imagine that you are already there.

Here are some of the images I made sure were part of my first vision board:

I wanted a beautiful home, so I put some pictures of both exteriors and interiors of houses that made me happy. (Interestingly, the home I ended up sharing with my parents and children looks very much like the one I imagined.)

I wanted to be represented by a modeling agency that believed in me, so I put a list of top modeling agencies along with their logos in a very visible location on my board.

I wanted to lose more than a hundred pounds, so I put up a photo of a model with a size 14 body and pasted my face on her body.

I wanted to be able to run around with my kids, so I showed a picture of a happy mother running through a park with her children.

I absolutely wanted to have far, far fewer financial worries, so I created a picture of a check made out to me for a million dollars and hung it up on my board. I also put a picture of me holding a sign that read, "DEBT FREE!"

I wanted to travel, so I hung stunning photographs of world capitals like Paris, Rome, and London, along with others of places like Hawaii and the Bahamas.

I wanted my children to be happy, so I hung photographs of them enjoying themselves.

I wanted to be featured in *People* magazine, so I hung a photograph of the magazine. (This is another one of my "visions" that came to be.)

I hung up quotes that I found inspiring and helpful. Here are some examples:

"Go confidently in the direction of your dreams. Live the life you have imagined."

"If you can't, you must. If you must, you can."

I also wanted to remind myself not to waste my time chasing unrealistic fantasies so I put up another quote that spoke to me: "If the door doesn't open, it's not your door." This quote has special meaning, because it helps me maintain a sense of peace and tranquility when things don't go my way. Sometimes we don't get what we think we want when we want it—and in my life, I've discovered again and again that this is for the best. In later years, I've gained clarity about why I didn't get what I wanted, and I always ultimately feel grateful.

I put my vision board on the wall at the foot of my bed so that I see it first thing when I wake up.

My vision board is incredibly helpful to me, and as my life progressed, I put work into creating a space that always kept my goals and aspirations front and center. Okay, over time, I got a little bit carried away, and in size, my vision *board* is now closer to a vision *wall*. Looking at it is the last thing I do at night and the first thing I do in the morning, and I continue to have an inspiring picture of what I want to achieve.

Every word and picture that hangs on my vision board is important to me. And as my life has improved and changed, I add new thoughts and images reflecting my growth and some of my newer goals. I want to have a clothing line as well as devote more time to life coaching, so I have photos of successful fashion lines as well as a list of potential clients and issues for life coaching. I also have a photo of Oprah, one of my heroes, on *Super Soul Sunday,* along with a photograph of myself. What a thrill it would be to appear with Oprah. I continue to love and rely on my vision board because it helps keep me excited and passionate about where I'm going and how my life is evolving.

Fiji

My first self-improvement seminar was so inspiring and life-changing that I wanted more. So I signed up for Robbins University, which offered intense mastery in different areas of my life and included a longer and more intensive seminar in Fiji. Let me repeat myself—Fiji! It was a life and wealth mastery retreat designed to help participants improve the quality of their lives, focusing on improving both health and finances. Well, I certainly needed help in both of these areas. My parents thought it would be a good thing for me to do (my father was very much in favor of the idea) and agreed to watch my children. I still can't believe that I signed up, and I'm still glad that I did. I think my experiences in Fiji helped me rev up my courage to do whatever was needed to improve my health—and that meant getting control of my weight. If I had not done that seminar, I don't know if I would have been able to sustain the focus and determination to move forward with weight loss surgery.

When I went to Fiji, I weighed about 375 pounds, which in itself made traveling a genuine challenge. Just getting to Fiji was scary, because for the last part of the journey, I was traveling on a small, very open island-hopper plane that seated eight. When I looked down at the water from my tiny seat, I couldn't help but think that I was going to fall off. I can't even begin to describe how much it terrified me.

Fiji was amazing; I swam in waterfalls wearing only shorts and a T-shirt. I even did most the climb up a fifty-foot pole and then jumped off with a bungee cord. Getting up close to the top of that pole at my weight—not to mention my fear of heights—was not easy. As I climbed higher and higher, holding on for dear life with sweaty palms, the weight of my backside and hips kept pulling me back, and it got harder and harder. My time in Fiji absolutely convinced me that I wanted new experiences more than I wanted food. I was hungry for life. Accomplishing what I did in Fiji gave me a new sense of freedom, which I needed badly, but it was mixed with an unshakeable awareness of how much my weight was holding me back. This was something I couldn't ignore. In Fiji I fell in love with the people and their lifestyle. I was inspired by my experience.

When I was recovering from my brain cyst, I went on a vegan diet, but I hadn't continued on that route. Being in Fiji, where there was such a strong emphasis on a holistic lifestyle, helped me open up and once again reorient myself to a healthier life. I began to think about a way to exercise regularly as well as find a better way of eating.

I left Fiji feeling like a new person with a better vision of myself and my future.

A Date with Destiny

My third Robbins self-improvement seminar occurred less than a year after Fiji, and it took place in Palm Springs, California. For me, more than anything else, this seminar helped me heal the hurt that I was carrying around with me as a result of various relationships in my life. I knew in my heart that at least some of my enormous weight gain had to do with hanging on to pain and surrounding myself with fat as a protective shield against life.

Thinking about my life, I began to understand how much I had tolerated because of my fear and dependency needs. Also, for the first time, I started to take ownership and responsibility for all my sh*t and my role in creating my problems. That seminar helped me realize that I needed to get more closure about my past. I needed to stop thinking about people and situations that caused me pain. I needed to forgive the past and the people who hurt me. I also needed to forgive myself. This was a major issue in my life.

One of my most unique experiences during the seminar was meeting Guru Singh, who was one of the seminar's featured guests. The first time I saw Guru Singh, standing there with his piercing blue eyes, wearing all white, including his white turban, he radiated so much magnetic energy that I wanted to go up and hug him. I knew that I was very much craving whatever he was able to feel. Later, during a meditation he was leading, he came over to me and passed his hands over my head. I immediately felt a vibration that was insane. Energetic waves of love, peace, and gratitude passed through my body. I didn't know that I was capable of feeling anything like that. I have continued to chase that feeling during my own meditations, but I've never again come close. But meeting Guru Singh intensified my commitment to my daily meditation. Doing so every morning helps clear my mind. My energy tends to bounce around, and daily meditation also helps keep me grounded.

Finding a More Spiritual Path

We are all searching for peace and happiness. For me, that means continuing to build a stronger connection to God and the universe. I am fortunate to have received so much support and love in my life—even if I haven't always recognized it at the time. However, if I said that I led a totally balanced life, I would be lying. I work at a variety of different jobs, which take time and effort. I often have to be in Los Angeles or New York City, which means travel. I have family who want me home with them, which is also where I want to be. And when you have children, there is always something that needs your time and attention—from a school event to a child with a cold. I have a variety of different work assignments. I make a point of doing certain things for myself, like working out and prepping my food and spending time in meditation and prayer. I try to go to church with my family every Sunday. I have friendships, work relationships, and relationships with other family members that require loving care. But I have little free time to do all the things I would like to do. My personal belief is that in life, you are always sacrificing something. That's just the way things work.

In short, I am dashing from place to place and hardly in a position to suggest how anyone finds balance. However, what works for me is understanding that I am willingly, and even happily, sacrificing one type of satisfaction for another. I'm grateful to have three wonderful children, work, siblings, and parents. And yes, a new love has entered my life. My life right now is one of peace and satisfaction.

Notice and Respond from the Heart

Have you received any divine messages today? As we make our way through life, I truly believe we are all regularly sent guidance and advice about what we can do to help us get where we are meant to be. Sometimes that help comes in the form of people who enter our lives to aid our decision-making or show us by example what it means to have a more spiritually evolved point of view. Sometimes this help comes when we least expect it from something we just happen to be reading—like an article in a magazine we pick up in the doctor's office that appears to speak directly to our current state of mind. I have often found real support and guidance from books that have helped me frame my attitude. And of course, reading the Bible is always a good way to lean into our faith.

We are all receiving messages and guidance. It can be something as simple as the little bird that shows up at your window, giving you a glimpse of God's divine and beautiful order, or it can be the person standing next to you on a line somewhere who happens to utter the words that instantly remind you of something you need to do. Sometimes the messages and guidance we receive are much more specific and pointed.

It's up to us to make sure we keep our hearts open and aware so we hear the messages we receive. And then, it's our job to respond appropriately. It's important that we pay attention to the divine messages in our lives. Ignore them, and we could head off in a foolish direction, as I have in the past. When we make the conscious decision to recognize the messages informing us of the help available in our daily lives. When we are in tune and connected, we start to walk the paths we are meant to walk. And everything flows.

CHAPTER 12

Showing Up for Yourself Is Showing Up for Others

PARENTHOOD IS A SHOCKING EXPERIENCE. NOTHING PREpares you for that moment when you are presented with a cute little squirmy person—unquestionably the most important being in the universe. Suddenly the only thing that matters is trying to keep your precious little baby satisfied and content. To do this, parents everywhere are prepared to give up everything else in their lives, including their personal comfort. Mothers know what this feels like: There is no longer any time to curl up to watch television or read a book; there will be no more chatting on the phone with friends; long, soothing showers or baths become distant memories;

and as far as uninterrupted sleep is concerned, just forget about it. I had no idea that my life could suddenly be so completely governed by the one overriding goal—Don't Let the Baby Cry! Nothing else mattered!

I was a young single woman without a partner, and when Bella, my oldest child, was born, I knew nothing about being a mother. Absolutely nothing! Soothing a baby, feeding a baby, bathing a baby—it was all foreign to me. The idea of changing a diaper was nothing short of terrifying! How about holding a baby? Suppose I dropped her?!

When I brought tiny little Bella home from the hospital, I was all alone because I'd lied to my parents, saying that I expected her father to be back from Mexico momentarily. "I'll be fine—don't worry," I told them. So there I was, depressed as well as scared out of my wits, with a brand-new infant—no partner, baby nurse, friend, or anybody else. Within two minutes of my father dropping me off and reluctantly walking out the door, my baby girl started crying, and I cried along with her. We were both wailing.

What was I going to do?

I guess I was going to have to figure it out. But it was slow going.

At first, I cried all the time, and whenever Bella cried, I cried even more and louder than she did.

It certainly didn't feel funny at the time, but I can't help but laugh when I remember one memory, a perfect example of incompetent new motherhood. Bella had started crying within minutes of being fed. I tried rocking her, pushing her in her carriage, and carrying her around the house. No matter what I did, she cried. And, as always,

I joined her and wailed along. I thought, Oh my God, she is in pain! Something serious could be wrong! I don't know what to do! I need help!

I absolutely thought it was a medical emergency—what else could it be?—so I dialed 911. The EMS team was great. One of the guys, who immediately realized I was as inept as I was hysterical, said, "Don't worry. It's going to be okay." He picked up little Bella and started burping her. Unlike me, he knew what he was doing.

Bella reciprocated with three giant burps. Then she gurgled happily. I felt like a total idiot. I also felt unbelievably frightened and helpless. I had a lot to learn.

What I remember best from the first two years of my daughter's life is that I was trying desperately to figure out how to be a good mom, and in the process, I forgot about most of my own needs. Thinking back over that time, although I was surrounded by my family, it sometimes seemed as though the only relationship that mattered was the one I had with my daughter. Most mornings, I dressed Bella and took her with me to my parents' office, first stopping in my mom's kitchen long enough to eat her large, wonderfully prepared breakfast—ham, eggs, refried beans, and sweet Mexican bread with cinnamon perfect for dipping into amazing dark coffee with sweet cream. It was easy to do my work while taking care of my daughter, who was surrounded by love as well as her toys and equipment. I was always happy that Bella received so much attention from my parents as well as my brother and sisters, who were still living at home.

Bella was my primary source of comfort and happiness. She went everywhere with me—a fixture on my hip or by my side. The high points of the week, probably for both of us, were the Mommy and Me art classes we took together every Wednesday and Friday. I have a very strong memory of Bella, both of us working with finger paint at a nearby art studio. My cute little toddler was significantly more talented than her mom. She loved looking at the colors and making careful decisions about which ones to use. Blue, red, yellow, green. She was so young, and yet she already had a basic understanding of what it means to mix colors and apply paint to paper. I loved watching her as she stopped to admire each hue. "Bootiful," she would say. "Bootiful" was one of her first words.

She was still on my hip when we first began dancing around the house together, and then it seemed as though almost as soon as she started walking, she also started dancing on her own—Gwen Stefani was an early favorite. She also loved having me read to her. Because I wanted Bella to be bilingual, I made a point of reading in Spanish as well as English and bought the classics like *Goodnight Moon* and *The Cat in the Hat* in both languages. Combining cultures was not always as easy as it might appear. The Mexican home remedies I loved didn't always match with American medical advice. I remember relatives telling me to give baby Bella chamomile tea with honey for tummy aches, but when I researched this remedy, there were very huge and specific warnings telling mothers not to give honey to babies until they were at least a year old. More than once I was faced with the dilemma of what to do when cultures clash.

For close to three years, Bella and I lived alone in our three-bedroom house, which sat on an acre of land. I loved that house, and most of my creative energy was spent decorating every single room so that it was different from the next. Some people might find this jarring, but for me it was fun and exciting to decorate each room so that it captured a different mood and color scheme. I grew up with a mother who preferred unadorned white walls and beige or navy carpets. As an adult, I craved art and color. Left to my own devices, I went crazy with colors, textures, and designs. The very modern main living room, which was filled with art by young local artists, had a red shag carpet and bright yellow Italian leather couches. The family room, which I called my John Lennon room, had a black leather sofa and black carpet and featured black-and-white artwork, including a large photo of John Lennon and Yoko Ono. In the dining room was an extremely long glass vintage table that seated fourteen. The chairs were black with very high backs. The dining room was the one pristine room that nobody used. Nobody ever ate at the dining room table, which was a good thing, because there was no way I would have been able to sit on the chairs.

As a child, I always wondered what it would be like to have pink walls. In my own adult house, I got to find out, and—for a while, at least—I became obsessed with pink. As you might imagine, my daughter's room was painted a sweet baby pink, with one accent wall in a hot neon pink. Her ceiling was pale blue with floating white clouds. Her full name, Isabella, was written out in colors of the rainbow on the walls over her bed. She had white curtains—decorated with pink hearts—on her windows. Her room was accented with Hello Kitty accessories, including Hello Kitty sheets, a Hello Kitty clock, and any other Hello Kitty add-ons I could find. Because I also loved pink and Hello Kitty, I picked up the theme in the kitchen—more pink walls along with another blue ceiling with floating white clouds and white marble counter tops. I loved my pink kitchen even though I didn't do much cooking in it.

When Bella was a baby, I worried about everything. Because I gained so much weight when I was pregnant and after my daughter was born, I was constantly worried about becoming diabetic and seriously thought I was going to pass away. I believe I was twenty-two when I got my first life insurance policy so she would have some security.

And then, of course, motherhood always seems to bring financial worries. I'm sure there are a few heiresses among us with no anxieties about paying for food, let alone winter coats, but for the most part, is there a single working mother anywhere who isn't worried about money?

Valentino

My daughter, Bella, was six when Valentino was born. He was a jaundiced, sickly, two-point-four-pound, unable-to-eat infant who needed a feeding tube. I was a depressed, recently rejected mom in strong pain from a C-section. Valentino had to stay in the neonatal unit until he weighed at least four pounds, which took a month. I had already lost his twin when I was pregnant and was worried sick about losing him. I stayed in the hospital almost round-the-clock. My father would relieve me for several hours a day so I could go home to shower and catch a quick nap on a real bed. But one of us was always there 24/7. Valentino was so small that my father could hold him in one hand. My father and Valentino share a strong and intense bond, which I believe started there in the NICU.

To say that my mother and father have been extraordinarily helpful with my children is a major understatement. Sitting with their single-mom daughter while she is giving birth to three separate children without a husband or partner in sight is certainly nothing they ever had in mind. But nobody could ever fault their family values, emotional strength, or capacity for love.

When Valentino came home from the hospital with a long list of instructions and concerns, my parents insisted that Bella and I move into their large house. I was very grateful to be in a protective environment, where parenting felt more manageable. If I wanted to take a shower or wash my hair, my parents were there to keep their eyes fixed on Valentino for the time it took. There were also so many strong memories of living with Anthony that I didn't want to be in my house anymore, so I said goodbye to the color scheme I loved, along with my underutilized Hello Kitty kitchen. In my parents' house, we made sure that Bella had another beautiful room. This time she decided how she wanted it decorated—lots of painted rainbows and clouds.

From the day Valentino was born, there were so many complications that motherhood took on a whole new meaning. I had to pay attention to everything. Was he eating enough? Was he peeing enough? Was his poop the right color? It was essential that I stayed on high alert. He seemed to stabilize when he was about three or four months old, and for a very short time, I thought he was going to be okay. Then he basically stopped developing. There was no strength in his body, and holding him was like carrying a rag doll. His head tilted to one side, and he didn't have enough strength to keep it up on his own. At five months, he had his first seizure. He was just sitting there in his chair, and then his eyes rolled back and reverted to a blank stare. It was terrifying to watch, and I had no idea what was happening. It lasted only thirty seconds or so, but they were the longest thirty seconds of my life. From that moment forward, I always feared another seizure. EMS taught me what to physically do when Valentino had seizures, but I continued to be concerned that I might be out of the room. What then?

After the seizure, Valentino began to get all kinds of tests. It was awful. I vividly remember the first time he had an MRI and had to be sedated. I was so worried and stressed.

There is nothing worse than seeing your child going through pain and discomfort. Then there were more tests and even fewer answers. Finally, when he was about seven months old, this rude ass of a doctor, who was totally lacking in compassion, gave me a diagnosis: mild cerebral palsy and atrophy of the brain. "Don't expect him to survive more than five years," he said. He was sure that Valentino had minimal life expectancy and that there would be little, if any, future development. According to this doctor, the only thing to do was to take my tiny little baby son home and make him as comfortable as possible.

When I left that doctor's office, I called my parents—pretty much a hysterical wreck. My father had an immediate response: "Start making appointments," he said. "Take him to different doctors and different hospitals. There has to be somebody who can help. You can't give up on your son."

"You Can't Give Up on Your Son"

My father's words stayed with me as I started doing research, frequently making long drives with Valentino to Los Angeles, San Francisco, and anywhere else that I thought might be able to provide advice or help. There were no real solutions, and it was quickly and amazingly apparent that traditional medicine was not the answer. We heard about stem cells as well as chelation therapy and finally decided that we would seek out treatments that were not available in this country, which almost immediately seemed to start having some positive results. Within a short time, Valentino began to make eye contact. This was a first, so we continued forward.

My parents and I did everything we could for Valentino, including a ton of physical therapy. I currently take him to physical therapy twice a week, and a private therapist comes to the house several other times. He is still prone to infections, so we are very careful about everything. Valentino's blood has been tested and retested many times—one of those tests indicated that he is both hypoglycemic and allergic to gluten. Now he is on a very strict diet, and we make sure that he eats every two hours.

Watching Valentino develop has been like watching a miracle unfold. It took years of work before he could lift his head on his own, let alone get around. His speech was seriously delayed; he didn't understand how to pick up food and was unable to grasp the concept of grabbing a Cheerio. When he was five and first able to point to something—a glass of milk—in order to communicate to me what he wanted, I broke down in tears. At that moment, I saw that all our work was paying off. Valentino, who is very smart, really worked hard to progress. He is a lesson in determination. When he was nine, Valentino was still only able to get around by crawling. At fourteen, he is now attending a regular school, where he uses a walker. He has a special curriculum and still needs an aide with him, but he has friends, a social life, and his own smartphone, which, like just about every child his age, he uses to play games. Although he still has a speech impediment, he has come a long way. He is incredibly strong and loving, a very good soul who loves having conversations and communicating with others. Valentino is always working hard, fighting to survive and be better. His faithful attitude and personality have made my entire family want to fight along with him.

Alex

My wonderful son Alex was born when Valentino was about a year and a half old. Alex looked healthy, but he was also premature, weighing two-point-six pounds at birth. Because of my experiences with Valentino, I was concerned about Alex, but he started to thrive almost immediately, quickly becoming a healthy, independent baby who soon slept through the night, which was good, because I was so worn down by taking care of Valentino and carrying two diaper bags that I don't think I could have managed a cranky baby. He did everything a baby is supposed to do enthusiastically and right on schedule. Alex's attitude toward life was like a present from God.

Alex's capacity to both defend and help out with his brother, Valentino, has always thrilled me. When Valentino was five, three-and-half-year-old Alex was the person who taught him slowly but surely how to crawl. The image that exists in my brain of Alex patiently helping his brother develop motor skills is one that makes me happy whenever I think about it. Already Alex is a young businessman. He intuitively seems to know how to make things happen. When he and his brother play games together, it's very apparent that he is motivating and teaching Valentino. Like his mom, Alex has a very competitive spirit. I see daily all the ways that Alex has helped Valentino step up and be part of the game.

At twelve, Alex is an all-around boy who loves life, video games, music, and dancing. He is good at math and was born with an entrepreneurial spirit. Give him something—anything—to sell, and he will pull out the appropriate app on his phone, and I will see that he is soon making a deal.

Learning to Appreciate Life's Beautiful Moments

In each of our lives, there are lovely and fragile moments that remind us of the beauty that can exist in human interactions. My children's relationships with one another have blessed me with many of these precious and remarkable times. The process of watching them grow and learn is filled with joy. But most moms can probably appreciate what I mean when I say that it's not always easy to take the time to relate to these lovely moments. So much is going on, and we all get so busy and stressed. We're trying to take care of our children's basic needs for food and shelter. We ask ourselves: Is the laundry done? Does everybody have clean and matching socks? The phone is ringing—do we take the call? Is it something important or another telemarketer trying to sell us solar panels?

A challenge we all face is learning to take the time to savor and be present for the beautiful moments in our lives. This has been a difficult lesson for me to learn. When something exceptionally good happens in my day-to-day life, I have often been too busy, too worried, or too stressed to fully enjoy the moment in time. I may have noticed that something special was taking place, but I didn't really let it sink in, and I didn't savor that moment. It's not just motherhood—I have done this in a variety of different areas in my life. I am sometimes more focused on my next activity—where I am going and what I have to do—than I am on the present. Living this way is a huge mistake; I'm working on this daily, to be present.

Living in the here and now is something we can learn from our kids. Children are almost always more present and focused on the moment than they are on yesterday's lingering problems or what they will be doing tomorrow or even in another hour. They are able to be happy and present, breathing in and savoring what they are doing. They get upset but can forget about what happened as though it never existed. As adults, we can develop the same kind of approach to our lives. Enjoy what's happening while it is happening. Look around you. Notice the smells, the sounds, the sights. Who are the people who are part of your life? Are you able to be present for them? Are you fully aware of what they are doing and thinking? Do you appreciate and enjoy them for who they are?

It's important that we all remember to savor the special moments in our lives. When these moments are gone, they are gone forever. We can train ourselves to be more present as we relate to the rest of the world—particularly our children. It's definitely worth doing.

The Loneliness of the Single Mother

I split from each of my children's fathers while still pregnant and gave birth to each of them without a significant other to hold my hand—all the while envying the other new moms who had partners by their sides. Each time I experienced the joy of becoming a mom to a new child, I also felt scared, sad, anxious, and profoundly alone. For many years I asked myself the same questions: Will I be able to be successful in raising my children on my own? Will my children suffer from the absence of another parent?

Yes, I was a single mom, but I was also a single mom for whom family is really important. Growing up in a close-knit family, I remember all those holidays and family trips. I have some exceptionally wonderful memories of being part of a family unit, and I wanted to replicate that for my kids; I can't help feeling guilty that I wasn't able to provide them with a traditional nuclear family. Being a mom alone with her children isn't always easy. Yes, there were joyous moments, but there were also times when I couldn't help but feel depressed and lonely, as well as isolated. When my brother got married, for example, I was the only one walking down the aisle without a partner by my side. At the reception, just about every cousin and distant family member decided it would be the perfect time to start a conversation with exactly the same question: "So why are you still alone?"

A couple of years ago, all of us—my brother and his wife, my sisters, their husbands, and all the kids—took a family trip to Disneyland. Each individual family unit was wearing special T-shirts designed for the trip. All the other kids were wearing shirts with names of both their parents. We all had a really great time, but I couldn't help but wonder whether my kids somehow felt deprived because they had only one parent with them. It was a joyful time, but there were still some isolated lonely moments that reminded me of what it felt like to give birth without a partner. I'm a woman—a strong woman. I have discovered that I can handle just about everything in my life. But there were so many times when I felt lonely and thought about what it would be like to have a strong man by my side sharing the joys, as well as the trials and tribulations, of parenthood.

Being a Single Parent: The Good Part

Do I think there are any advantages to being a single mom? If I'm being honest, I would probably say yes. I sometimes see husbands and wives disagreeing about how to handle parenting decisions and I think, Well, at least I never had to do that.

I'm also acutely aware of the almost impossible task of being a woman trying to balance kids, career, and a husband. I feel nothing but admiration for all the women struggling to do this.

I think about what's going on in my life on a daily basis. I often have to rush out the door to get to an audition, and the kids are calling out,

"Mom, Mom, Mom, I can't find my homework!"

"Mom, Valentino needs help!"

"Mom, my uniform isn't ironed!"

"Mom, when are you going to be back? I need you to pick me up from practice."

"Mom, can you listen to what I wrote?"

"Mom, I think my phone is broken. Can you get it fixed?"

Certainly, with the right partner the tasks and caretaking would be shared, and that would be a wonderful thing. But being a single mom is preferable, I think, to being married to someone abusive, controlling, or as needy as a kid. It's nice to call the shots, without consulting another person on how the thermostat should be adjusted or how household chores should be divided. Who takes out the garbage? Who's making the coffee? There is a limit to how many things I can think about or debate. From my work as a life coach and being on a television show that addressed people's problems, I know that some women are living with partners who actually compete with the children for attention. That's a nightmare I would never want to address.

Having said all that, I must admit that throughout all my single years, I always carried the hope in my heart of being able to have a good, solid relationship resembling the one my parents share.

Figuring Out What Makes Your Child Feel Loved

We are all the results of complex genetic and environmental influences. I see this in my children, who have such different talents and approaches to the world. As a mom, part of the job is figuring out what's important to each of your children and what they want from their relationships. One of my children responds best to affection; another to communication and talking; a third just wants quality time—it doesn't matter how it's spent.

Your children also tend to be different as they go through different stages. You think you have it all figured out, and then suddenly your child changes. The little girl who wanted to be surrounded by pink and to wear only dresses now informs you that she hates pink and will wear only jeans. The boy who craved affection and togetherness suddenly wants nothing but "space" and more alone time. Keeping up with your children as they change and grow is an ongoing challenge.

An important part of our jobs as parents is knowing who our children are and what makes them feel loved. It's up to us to figure out each child's individual love language. What makes your children feel loved? Have you ever asked them? Have you ever asked what you, as their parent, can do to make them feel more loved? Do they want more time, more affection, more conversation, more understanding? Do they crave your presence? Do they want you to spend more time talking with them about the things that are important to them? Do they want you to use words to affirm and support what they are doing on a day-to-day basis?

When I asked my children, their responses were interesting as well as different. They all wanted more conversation and quality time. One of my children responds best to physical affection; another likes to talk, talk, talk and feels most loved when I listen, listen, listen. I know that as a child I craved words of love and support. My father grew up in an environment in which few people said “I love you” to their children. What he learned is what he did; so he didn’t say it, and I always missed hearing those words from my male role model. I learned the importance of saying the word, and, as a parent, I now constantly tell my children how much I love them. And, as he grew older, my dad completely changed. With my children, who he adores, he has no problem saying “I love you.”

Self-Esteem and the Plus-Size Parent

When my children were small, I was so large that there were many things I wasn’t able to do with them. This was absolutely the single most important issue motivating me to lose weight. I love being active and having fun, and I wanted to have fun with them.

But there was another factor that I couldn’t ignore. I was teased and downright bullied as a child because of my weight—and all of this seriously affected my self-esteem. I hadn’t thought much about how my weight was impacting my children’s self-esteem until my son

Alex was about seven. As I did every day, I was driving him to school. The very moment we pulled up to the curb near the entrance, he jumped out of the car. I started to get out with him, but he stopped me. "Please, Mom," he said, "don't come in there with me." It turned out the other kids were making fun of my hip size and, consequently, of him, every time I walked him to his classroom door.

Knowing about my self-esteem issues, I am always very concerned about what I might have passed on to my children. I know they feel my energy. I always remember one day when some upsetting memories brought tears to my eyes. I thought I was hiding what I was feeling, but then little Alex came over to me and used his hand to wipe my tears. When he was finished, he showed me that his hand was wet. So much for thinking that you can hide your emotions from your children!

I try very hard to address self-esteem issues with my children and encourage them to talk about and work through the things that might make them feel bad about themselves. I try very hard to make sure that my kids have great self-esteem, no matter what their challenges. I don't want them to shut down; I want them to be able to stand tall and handle criticism. I've tried to teach them to let go of negative criticism and instead build on the positive.

My children each have different concerns. Bella had a much better high school experience than I ever did. She was vice president of her class and a cheerleader and has the social skills necessary to fit into any group. Unlike me when I was growing up, she has dozens of friends and is not in hiding. I've tried to make sure she feels empowered and beautiful, but I can't help but identify with some of the things she will face as she takes her own journey. When she was still a little girl, I remember her looking at Valentino and crying, "What's wrong with my brother? What can I do to help him?" She is just starting college and wants to train for a career as a psychologist—helping children.

Alex has always been a confident boy, but he knows what it feels like to have a bully attack him. Recently he told me that another boy called him a "fat Mexican." Alex told me, "I'm proud to be Mexican." Alex said that he replied to the boy, "I am Mexican, and why do you have an issue with my weight?" Talking to me, Alex said, "I know who I am and what I am, and I was happy that I was able to stick up for myself." When somebody says something unkind to Alex, he knows how to respond by saying, "That's your opinion," and then moves on with his life. I pray that Alex always continues to value himself.

Valentino knows that he does things differently from the other kids and is accustomed to people staring at him. He has learned to smile at them when they do this. The other day, some guy was staring at him, and Valentino turned toward him, smiled, and said, "Have a good day, sir." I was so proud of his ability to do this.

I know all the ways in which my issues with self-esteem led to bad decision-making. It goes without saying that I am always on alert, trying to make sure that my children feel confident and valued. I don't want them to make mistakes that can be directly attributed to low self-esteem. Every day, in every way possible, I work hard to show them that they need to validate themselves. I know from my own life that my lack of self-validation is the reason why I looked for approval from others and in the process made some genuinely stupid decisions.

Learning to Shut the F*ck Up, Pay Attention, and Listen

As long as my children are doing what I want them to do, of course I'm happy. The problem is that, from their point of view, doing exactly what I want may not make them happy. We have to love our kids for who they are and who they may become. It's very tempting to try to push our children to follow the interests we decide are best for them, but it may not be what they want for themselves. If we hope to have better relationships with our kids, paying attention to what they are saying and what they think is important. This is part of the process of validating our children. We have to do more asking about their lives—what they are doing, feeling, and experiencing—and less lecturing about what we think they should be doing, feeling, and experiencing. Kids know when their parents are present and paying attention, so don't think you can fool them.

It can be very difficult to be a child today. They are under so much pressure, both social and academic. We don't always know the half of what's happening during those hours when they are away from us. And they don't always tell us. My parents never knew everything that was happening in my life. I remember when I was about nine or ten, I went up to my teacher's desk to ask a question. She responded by grabbing me by my ponytail and pulling me across the room back to my seat. I never told anybody. I thought I had done something wrong and was embarrassed by what had happened. I think most teachers today realize they can't act out physically, but they still say things that are hurtful. Kids are exposed to all kinds of experiences that hurt their shining spirits. As parents, we need to be accomplished detectives to make sure we know what's happening. To do this we need to spend more time listening to them talk about their interests, fears, failures, and friends.

As much as we are discovering who our kids are, they are discovering themselves. A large part of our parental responsibility involves helping them do just that so they can become the very best versions of themselves. That's what we want for them.

Watching Your Children Become More Independent Is a Scary Process

Allowing your children to become more independent may be one of the most difficult things you can do as a parent. My mother—who is undeniably right up there among the most loving, giving, sacrificing, amazingly wonderful moms who ever lived—and I still clash because she is happiest when I am home, safe and sound, with her. I feel the same way about my children. But I also know from my history of rebelling that sometimes when you don't let your children make their own decisions and move away naturally, you may end up with an extremely rebellious son or daughter.

My daughter, for example, is talking about the possibility of spending a semester studying in Europe. It fills my heart with terror. Yet I know that if she does decide to do that, it's important that

I be able to support her. Her journey is not my journey. She is close to adulthood, and my role as her mom is evolving. I have to stop hovering and telling her what to do. Instead, I have to respect what she wants, let her live her life, and stand by her.

As parents, we all need to understand that our children may want to lead lives that are different from our own. They may end up with a completely different view of the world—not to mention different politics—but this is their choice. And, yes, I am sometimes going to become upset at my children's choices. But I know that I am going to have to respect their opinions and decisions. All you can try to do is develop respectful relationships with your children so that all of you are able to discuss your concerns. That's it. I also realize that whatever paths my children walk, I'll be walking with them, because nothing happens to our kids that doesn't also happen to us. Nonetheless, I want all my children to become independent, loving adults. None of us ever finds out what we are capable of accomplishing until we start moving forward on our own.

Forgiving Yourself for Being Human

Living with me as a parent hasn't always been easy for my kids. I'm definitely overly emotional. I've been depressed about life, worried about money, anxious about tomorrow, and, sometimes, angry for a variety of reasons, including something one of the kids is doing.

When I lose it with one of my children, which of course I do, I am often overwhelmed with feelings of remorse and guilt. Why couldn't I have been more patient? Why couldn't I have been calmer and more understanding?

As parents, we sometimes need to learn to be easier on ourselves. We need to realize that the perfect parent doesn't really exist. Good parenting is about keeping our intentions honest and knowing that we are doing the best that we can. Good parenting is about love, acceptance, and being a reliable and trustworthy witness to our children's journeys. We're teaching each other.

Showing Up for Yourself Is Showing Up for Others

If there was one piece of advice I could give to others, particularly parents, it would be to remind them to take care of themselves. It's like what they tell you on airplanes: You have to put the oxygen mask on yourself first before you can help anybody else. Many of us have been indoctrinated to believe that people who take care of themselves are being selfish. Who the hell thought up this myth? It's not selfish to show up for yourself; it's realistic and life-affirming. So cut yourself some slack. Find time for yourself, and don't feel guilty when you do so. Promise yourself that you will make room in your schedule for something that makes you happy. Nurture your interest in poetry class, pottery, or dance. Take the time to research classes that are being offered at the community center. Whether it's gardening, knitting, painting, sculpture, or anything else, find a creative project that brings you joy. Don't be afraid to go out to lunch or dinner with friends. If you can't afford babysitters, look for other good moms with whom you can trade time.

Don't put off satisfying your needs. Many parents always assume that they will be able to catch up and do some of the things they want "tomorrow." But life doesn't work that way, and you can get into the habit of putting off "tomorrow" indefinitely. By remembering your needs and taking care of yourself, you will be making yourself happier today. And being happy vastly increases the possibility that you will have happy kids. Happiness is contagious. Happy people make the people around them, including their children, feel happier as well.

Self-care is not a negotiable. It's not a luxury, and it's not selfish. This is something I learned the hard way, but you don't have to. Keep in mind that if you are not making your own self-care a priority, you will feel drained and exhausted. Then you will almost inevitably start feeling resentful and start complaining. This is going to create negative energy in your family. And then nobody feels good. If you don't feel good about yourself, don't expect others to feel or act differently.

Remember that you can't give what you don't have, and none of us can give from an empty cup. So help keep your cup full by putting a priority on your own joy and well-being. And share your good feelings with others.

CHAPTER 13

Stop Looking for Love

AFTER I STARTED MODELING, A WOMAN NAMED JASMINE friended me on Facebook and every now and then would send me positive comments or messages. In recent years, she could see from my posts that I was traveling regularly to Los Angeles for work.

"Hey, that's where I live. We should get together for dinner," she messaged me.

"Sounds like fun," I messaged back.

We were originally planning to meet on a Wednesday, just the two of us, but I had to work late, so I asked to change it to Friday and agreed that I would stop by her house on my way back to Vegas. Los Angeles to Las Vegas is a long drive—about four to six hours, depending on the traffic—but I'm very accustomed to doing it. So on Friday, instead of trying to find something healthy to eat at a fast food restaurant while on my way home, I would be having dinner with Jasmine. It sounded good to me.

Friday morning I received a Facebook message from Jasmine. It said, "My sister and her husband will be here, and I thought we could all go out for sushi. Is that okay? Would you mind if my brother joins us?"

Good question. I had already learned through several Facebook exchanges that Jasmine's brother was Gilbert, my first boyfriend back when I was a teenager. Gilbert, who came and sat on my front porch with me under my father's spotlight and stroked my hand and kissed my cheek when he was sure my parents weren't looking. Gilbert, who went off saying he would return, but who got married instead. *That* Gilbert!

Did I mind if Gilbert was also there for dinner? Truth be told, I had always wondered about Gilbert. What had happened to him? And why hadn't he taken the time to break up with me more appropriately?

Jasmine and her sister, Alejandra, and their husbands were waiting for me when I arrived, and we had a nice time talking, but where was Gilbert? Was he late, or was he not showing up? He probably doesn't want to see me, I thought to myself. Well, Gilbert ended up being more than twenty minutes late. When he came in, he gave me a hug. I swear, when he touched me, I got butterflies in my stomach, just as I had when I was a teenage girl. I looked at him and saw how he had changed. His jet-black hair had started to turn gray but he was still very handsome in khaki jeans and a black polo—and he smelled so good.

"Excuse me," he said. "Can I talk to you outside alone for a minute?"

Once we got in the yard, he told me that he was late because he had been sitting in his car in the driveway—he was nervous about seeing me and still felt bad about what had happened between us when we were both so much younger.

"Before we go to dinner," he said, "I wanted to have a chance to apologize for what I did twenty years ago. I can't tell you how often I've thought of you and how much guilt I felt about the pain I may have caused you by walking away like that. I am so sorry."

There are many times in life when we are waiting for an apology that never comes. In Gilbert's case, I knew how much he had hurt me when I was a young teenage girl completely smitten by a tall, thoughtful, and sensitive boy. And he always remained in my thoughts, not only because I had liked him so much. He had been the first guy to kiss me as well as the first guy to cheat on me. His actions had a huge impact on my capacity for trust. How could I forget any of that? But Gilbert actually apologized. He remembered and acknowledged the experience. He said, "I'm sorry," and he didn't pretend that nothing had happened or that it was no big deal. Gilbert also told me that he was divorced and, in the love and romance department, it hadn't all turned out so perfectly for him either. He shared that he had paid his own price for what he did.

I looked at Gilbert, and I told him how much I appreciated his apology. I didn't anticipate it, but it was closure, and it felt good.

After dinner, we returned to his sister's house, where she brought out pictures of Gilbert and me from twenty years before. I had never seen them and in fact didn't know they existed, but Gilbert had given them to his sister for safekeeping. As I was preparing to leave, I said that I was accustomed to the long drive, but if anybody was certified, I could probably use some CPR for extra energy on the road. Hearing this, Gilbert walked over and kissed me, just as he had on my father's porch. Once again—Muchas Mariposas! Racing hearts, racing thoughts: *Holy sh*t, Gilbert is kissing me!* He and I made a date for the following week, when I would be back in LA. At first I wasn't sure where our relationship would be headed, but when I saw him for the second time, I knew in my heart of hearts that we had a special connection, and my almost immediate gut reaction was *Gilbert and I are going to get married.*

Gilbert proposed a few months later on the evening of December 23. Once again, we were at his sister's house. Once again, he pulled me out into the yard alone. It was a cool, clear night with a star-studded sky. Gilbert got down on one knee and asked, "Rosie, will you marry me?"

I was very nervous about telling my parents, worried that they would say something along the lines of, "What kind of crazy sh*t is she doing now?" But my father simply nodded, and my mother said, "I always knew he was the one."

We were married by my parents' longtime pastor in a simple but elegant private ceremony in Vegas with our families in attendance. Gilbert had my wedding ring inscribed GILBERT AND ROSIE SONG OF SOLOMON 3:4. The Song of Solomon quote reads, in part, "For I have found the one my soul loves."

And so a page was turned. Today Gilbert and I couldn't be happier, and we are the proud parents of Emiliano, a brand new baby boy.

The Challenges of Finding Love

Yes, I found love, but getting there was a long, twisting path. Finding a healthy, satisfying relationship is challenging for everybody—no matter what size you are wearing. But is it harder for plus-size women? Certainly a large number of curvy women would say no because they are in solid, reliable relationships with people who love and adore them. But too many others complain bitterly about the limited number of available partners who want to waltz off into the sunset with plus-size women.

By now, I feel as though I'm somewhat of an authority on the special problems plus-size women face when trying to find or maintain loving relationships. I know that I always wanted a strong marriage like the one my parents share. Anyone who looks at my relationship history can quickly figure out that for many years, this was an elusive goal. However, my parents' example was always a saving grace. Because I had seen how a genuinely good and committed relationship works, I was always able to quickly leave relationships when there was infidelity. I know that relationships take work, and I'm more than prepared to do that work, but there are three things I won't tolerate—the Three As: Addiction, Abuse, and Adultery. I don't want those in my life. Who does?

As a plus-size woman, I also know all too well some of the emotionally and even physically abusive situations that can arise. I remember trying to talk to my then husband Marcos about having a media career. "Are you crazy?" he asked. "I'll be dead before you ever get a job like that!"

I still remember wondering, If he loves me, why doesn't he love my body, and why doesn't he believe in me?

Please don't get me wrong. There are many men who appreciate full-figured women. But sometimes those men are embarrassed to admit it and don't appreciate them when anybody else is around.

Before I had even turned sixteen, I had met guys who were comfortable talking to me only when nobody else was watching. I continued to meet men like this throughout my life.

I met Michael, for example, when I was working in New York City. When we met, my modeling career had already taken off, and I was very happy that he asked me out because he was interesting and I loved talking to him. When we were alone together, he was extremely affectionate and attentive. But as soon as other people were nearby, it seemed to me that his attitude changed. One beautiful late afternoon on a Sunday in mid-December, I convinced him to go with me for a walk. I always had a fantasy about strolling down Fifth Avenue hand in hand with a man and looking at the Christmas windows. The day itself fulfilled my dreams: A light snow was falling, the lights in the holiday windows were sparkling, and I was with a man I liked. All he had to do was hold my hand, and my fantasy would be realized. But it never happened. I decided to overcome my natural shyness and tentatively reached out to touch his hand. He responded by pulling away, crushing my fantasy. At that moment, the possibility of a romance between us died. I knew this guy liked me, but it was hideously apparent that he only liked me in private. In public, whenever he was anywhere where he might possibly be seen by colleagues, it was a different story. He made me feel as though he was ashamed to be with me. If I wasn't plus-size, would he have reached to hold my hand in public? Wasn't I worthy of love, regardless of my dress size? Thinking about that day still pisses me off.

Appreciating Men Who Like Curvy Women

Some men like Asian women. Some men prefer Latina women. Some men choose African American women. Some are automatically attracted to blue-eyed blondes; others are drawn to short women with dark hair. There are all kinds of people, and they are attracted to all kinds of romantic partners. But why is it that a man who chooses plus-size women is given a label? One of the terms for such men we hear used most often these days is "chubby chaser."

Calling a guy a chubby chaser almost makes it seem as though there is something wrong with him. Women who prefer heavier men are sometimes also called chubby chasers, but they are less likely to be shamed. But whether you are talking about a man or a woman, it's an unnecessary label that tells us nothing about all the subtle and beautiful interactions that take place in intimate and loving relationships.

I personally am happy to see that men who like curvier women are beginning to come out of the closet about their preferences. But I also can't help but be aware that they are being treated shabbily. They are frequently stigmatized and sometimes even ostracized. Their friends, for example, may make fun of them, saying things like, "What the f*ck's wrong with you—you like a fat girl?" I heard that kind of thing when I was in high school. Small wonder that so many men are embarrassed about liking curvy women! We are all real people with real personalities, interests, and preferences—all of us want love and happiness. Calling someone names is as dehumanizing as it is unkind.

We live in a world that, for the most part, values political correctness as well as kindness. We get upset when we hear others being insulted because of their ethnic or racial origins. It's not right, and we don't want to be part of this kind of mean-spirited behavior. With good reason, the media and entertainment industry now censors much of this intolerable cruelty. This is not true about how it treats people who are overweight. Fat jokes still abound everywhere. Comics still make fun of people who are fat. We see skits featuring larger men and women doing pratfalls, and people laugh. Nothing seems to have ever conveyed the message that it is hurtful to laugh at people who are larger in size. I think we need to keep this in mind and applaud those individuals who are strong enough to follow their romantic preferences without worrying about what others will think or say.

And What the F Is a "Feeder"?

I will never forget Daniel. I was on the subway in New York City when I saw him staring at me. A tall guy with beautiful brown eyes, he was wearing a fabulous and very stylish suit. I had hopped on a subway to get to a downtown location for a *Curvy Girls* shoot. We both got off the subway at the same stop. And then—would coincidences never end?—we both began trying to hail a cab, not the easiest thing to do on a crowded New York City street corner. He caught the first cab. "Where are you heading?" he asked with a smile.

I was going to a location in Greenwich Village, and I told him the cross streets. It was probably less than half a mile away, but I was wearing very high heels and I also didn't know how to get there. "Come on," he said, "it's on my way. I'll drop you."

It took him maybe four traffic lights to ask for my phone number. "I'll call you tonight," he promised. And he did.

As we talked on the phone, he told me he was an accountant who was in the middle of a divorce.

"Are you sure about that?" I asked.

He laughed. "When we meet for dinner," he told me, "I'll show you proof."

We talked again the following night, and then, the following night. I told him that I had always wanted to take a carriage ride in Central Park. "Let's do that before dinner," he suggested.

Because I love Central Park, sitting in a carriage behind a horse trotting through the park was incredibly exciting to me. I was beginning to really like Daniel for arranging this little adventure. During the ride, he asked me about myself and also told me more about himself—hopes, aspirations, career—all the usual first-date stuff.

When we got to the restaurant, he reached into his inside jacket pocket and pulled out an envelope that contained copies of legal documents that referred to his divorce. "I just want you to know," he said, "that I am on the up-and-up."

Were there any glaring red flags? Okay, as we ate, I did notice that he seemed to be paying much too much attention to watching me chew. Okay, and he may have practically swooned when I buttered a piece of bread and put it in my mouth. What did I think? I don't know. I guess I thought he liked my face. This was all good.

We had a lovely dinner. Then he insisted on dessert. "This place has the best cheesecake," he said. I was trying to lose weight, but he seemed determined to get me to try some cheesecake, so I went along with it.

"Just one piece—we'll share it," I told him.

When the waiter placed the cheesecake in the center of the table, Daniel pushed it toward me. "Try it," he said.

I took a bite.

"Yum," I said.

My date smiled.

"Will you eat a cheesecake for me?" he asked with more intensity than made me happy. "Will you eat it slowly?"

"What the . . . F?"

At that time, I had never even heard of feeders. But Daniel was one of them. And he creeped me out! I made some kind of excuse to end the date as soon as dinner was finished. At my hotel, I dashed into the lobby. "Thank you for a terrific evening," I said as I scampered toward the elevator. Later, back in my room, I got on my computer and I looked up "men who like to watch you eat." There were dozens of stories from women who told about gaining weight because of partners who practically force-fed them.

When Does a Preference Become a Fetish?

By the time I entered the dating world, I had three children, but I was still *so* naïve about some things. But almost as soon I put my toe into the world of the "single and searching," I quickly started to hear some stuff that I found strange at best. One man with whom I had exchanged no more than a few words actually looked at me and said, "I wonder how your fat feels and how it shakes when you move, because that really turns me on."

As I walked away, I looked at him and said, "I am so out of here."

In recent years, more and more has been discussed and written about men who are described as having a fetish about fat. A few years back, I was modeling in Full Figured Fashion Week in Paris, and I became aware of several well-dressed older men who were there ogling women modeling lingerie. I've never modeled lingerie, but as I was standing there, I heard a man tell one of the models that he admired her cellulite. He then smiled at her and said, "I particularly love the roll of fat underneath your bra line."

I could see that the model was extremely uncomfortable with what he was saying. Was this really a compliment? Was he actually being sincere, or was he being sarcastic? She clearly didn't know how to respond. I didn't know what to think either. Was he a man who had a fat fetish and was he simply being open about showing it? And if he was, was that a good thing, a bad thing, or simply a confusing thing?

If you search the internet, you will quickly discover that people are more and more open about having a fat fetish, and new ways of expressing fat fetishes are cropping up regularly. Some men actually fantasize about being squashed by much larger women sitting on their faces or bodies. Squashing would appear to be a form of sadomasochism in which the man enjoys feeling actual pain because he doesn't have enough oxygen.

I sort of understand that people are turned on by a variety of different stimuli. For myself, however, this approach holds absolutely no appeal. I want a relationship based on mutual love—not fetishism. I don't want to be judgmental here, but for me, I'm freaked out and turned off by the idea of a man who is more interested in touching a fold of fat than he is in discovering who a woman is and learning more about her thoughts and feelings.

Self-Esteem and Body Shaming

A high percentage of women know what it is to lack confidence about their bodies. Any woman who has ever been insulted, or made to feel insecure about the size of her hips, arms, breasts, stomach, or thighs is likely to have self-esteem issues. It's difficult to feel good about yourself if you have memories of being insulted or even teased about your hips or breasts on the school playground or locker room. But the problems of being body shamed don't stop when we get out of school. As I've personally learned, our problems with self-esteem inevitably spill over and have a strong impact on our romantic relationships throughout our entire lives.

Here's a fact: Women with low self-esteem are more likely to make questionable relationship choices and decisions than women who have a more positive view of themselves. If you have a history of getting involved with men who aren't good *to* you or good *for* you, and you want your life to change, the first thing you need to think about is improving your self-esteem. A woman with a strong sense of self-worth is more likely to attract good partners and avoid those who won't treat her with the respect and acceptance she deserves.

Nobody is born with low self-esteem. If you are challenged in this area, it is because of all the memories that reside in your brain pinging with great regularity, telling you that you are less than perfect. I was so frequently bullied about the size of my butt that at age sixteen, I remember honestly asking myself, *Who would fall in love with a girl who has a body like mine*? Now, of course, I wonder why I had such a negative view of myself.

I suppose there must be some women who were never made to

feel insecure about their bodies. Nobody ever said or did anything that made them feel deeply flawed. But this is rarely the case. We all live in a time where we are bombarded by messages from media and the rest of the outside world that beauty is primarily packaged in small sizes. The women depicted as desirable in films, television, and advertisements are almost always thin and perfectly proportioned. That's not how it is in the real world, where it's estimated that the average American woman is a size 16, but it's how it is in the media world that influences how we feel about ourselves and those around us.

How Low Self-Esteem Causes Problems in Relationships

I've given a great deal of thought to how my lack of self-esteem impacted my relationships. Here's some of what I've learned about myself and other women like me:

> Because women with low self-esteem lack confidence, they look to the outside world to bolster their self-worth. This makes them very vulnerable to manipulative partners. When they meet men who say all the things they are hoping to hear, they fail to maintain appropriate boundaries. When I was younger, this made me very vulnerable to the wrong men. I learned the hard way that a large number of the guys who say all the things you want to hear—often before they even know you—can be less than sincere. They just know which buttons to push to get you to agree to whatever they want at the moment.

Women with low self-esteem typically have problems with self-acceptance. They may have regular interior dialogues in which they criticize themselves. Then, if they get involved with abusive partners who are experts at finding ways to put women down, it can feel more familiar than it does threatening or scary.

Women with low self-esteem are often way too eager to please and end up doing most of the emotional, and even physical, work involved in maintaining a relationship. Almost inevitably they do more than their fair share.

Women with low self-esteem frequently believe they are unworthy. Believing this about yourself helps create relationships that are lopsided and less than equal.

Women with low self-esteem are likely to be more willing to overlook a partner's problems. They actually think things like, "I accept so many of his failings. That should make him overlook mine—including my crazy family, credit card debt, and, yes, of course, my weight."

Women with low self-esteem are typically anxious to fit in and belong. Because of this, we can fail to be self-protective and maintain strong, healthy boundaries. We are much too hesitant to stick up for ourselves. For a long time in my life, I went along with what others wanted. I learned the hard way that saying no sometimes is a way of protecting and caring for your own well-being.

Women with low self-esteem frequently say they have difficulty meeting potential romantic partners. Their insecurity causes them to avoid social events, so they spend

> little time out in the real world, where they might meet real people.
>
> Women with self-esteem issues tend to accept people who are giving them less than they deserve—and all too often find themselves in relationships with hurtful partners who mirror the negative voices and experiences of their past and confirm their own inner dialogues.

From my own experience, I think it's wise for women to understand that they may have self-esteem issues. This means there's work to do: on how we feel about ourselves, and how to maintain appropriate and healthy boundaries; on knowing when and how to say yes or no. We need to do whatever is necessary to honor our sense of self-worth. Some women may want to see a therapist or coach to help with this work.

Bottom line: We all have to spend at least as much time on our own inner and spiritual growth as we do on trying to please others. If you don't take care of yourself, nobody else will. And the journey starts by healing from the inside out. We show others how to treat us by the way we treat ourselves. If you are not receiving the love and respect you deserve, I encourage you to look inward and heal those thoughts not in alignment with the relationships you want to attract. It is by making the unconscious conscious that you come to develop healthy relationships that originate from your authentic self.

Stop Looking for Love

I had often heard people say things like, "Stop looking for love and wait for it to find you." For a long time, I didn't get it, but after thinking about my attitude and behavior in several failed relationships, I began to understand. When I was younger, I was consumed with the idea of finding love and getting married. As far as I was concerned, that was the only thing that mattered. When I met a potential romantic partner, I was prepared to do whatever I had to do to become the person he needed me to be. But by my mid-thirties, I had reached a new and better understanding. I was successful and happy with my life, and finding love had stopped being my number one priority.

It's important to me that you understand what I mean when I tell you to stop looking for love. I don't mean that you should give up on love and close yourself down to the possibility of finding it. Love is an important part of life, and we need to remain open to it. We all want to love and be loved. What I don't want you to do is to become so obsessed with having a relationship that you lose sight of who you are, what you need, and where you are going.

Among other things, women who want to find love more than anything else can appear desperate. They are so eager that they jump into relationships too quickly and ignore behavior that is unacceptable. I don't want to see you get your heart broken and waste your precious time trying to find love in all the wrong places, such as relationships that aren't working. I learned through hard experience that you can't force love, and you can't love a man into loving you. You can be the best woman in the world, but if you are doing way more than your share of work to maintain the relationship, it's not meant to be. You should be with someone who is investing as much in the relationship as you are.

If you are not getting what you need from a romantic partner, stop trying to make it happen. Know when it's time to cut your losses, face the fear, and walk away. Also, stop forgiving abuse, infidelity, or hurtful behavior. Don't let the other person become comfortable with disrespecting you. The more often you keep taking somebody back, the less respect they will have. You don't want to spend your life with partners who repeat hurtful behaviors because they depend on your forgiveness and don't consider the possibility that they might lose you or destroy the relationship.

Here's a quote I love:

> *Whatever comes, let it come. Whatever stays, let it stay. Whatever goes, let it go.*
>
> H. W. L. POONJA (PAPAJI)

Finally, put more of your great energy into building your self-esteem by exploring your creativity and finding things you love to do for yourself.

Here are some suggestions:

Learn to enjoy going places alone. People with low self-esteem can find it difficult to be content spending time by themselves because they rely on drawing energy from others. They use others to position and define themselves. Remind yourself that being alone is not the same as being lonely. Sometimes spending time in your own company is the right remedy for improving your life.

We all have interests. What are yours? Do you love music, art, dance? Find a class that will give you pleasure and encourage your creativity.

Date yourself. Take yourself out to dinner, lunch, or even brunch. Go to a movie, play, concert, or lecture. Choose places and events that you really think you would enjoy. When you are out on your date with yourself, don't forget to remind yourself how amazing and lovable you are.

Since the relationship you have with yourself is the only one you can't leave, you might as well pour tons of love into it.

CONCLUSION

What You Go Through, You Grow Through

MANY OF US HAVE SEEN PHOTOS OF HOLLYWOOD'S ICONIC Melrose Gate with the palm trees rising high above the two arches and *Paramount Pictures* written out in script. This is where thousands of amazing movies and television shows, everything from *Forrest Gump* to *Cheers* to *NCIS: Los Angeles,* have been made. When I saw Melrose Gate, I almost couldn't believe it was real. I always remember one of the first times I was there to shoot *Face the Truth,* a television show for which I was a co-host. As I drove through security, the guard said, "Good morning, Ms. Mercado!" That's when it hit me: Holy sh*t! I'm actually working here! This is not a mistake! This is really where I am supposed to be.

We each need to own what happens in our lives—the great, the good, the bad, the ugly, and the unexpected. I have had to own up to my fair share of mistakes in life. And now, I have to ask myself: How did I, a Latina woman who once weighed 420 pounds, end up first working as a model and then as a life coach who appears on nationally televised talk shows? How did all this happen? And because I know we each have a purpose in this life, I also need to ask, "*Why* did this happen?"

It never had been a dream of mine to become a life coach. I think the first person who suggested I should become one was a producer on one of the television shows I appeared on after my weight loss.

"Did you ever think of becoming a life coach?" she asked.

Well, no, I never had. But then the logic of taking that step dawned on me. My eyes opened up to the possibility, and I became very excited and determined. In many ways I felt I had spent a lifetime preparing for this role. The various problems I have faced made me significantly more aware and sensitive of other people's challenges and more compassionate about their problems and issues.

My firm belief is that everything happens for a reason, even if we don't understand it at the time. We are here to learn and grow from our personal challenges, and I have learned that there is a great deal of wisdom wrapped around our pain. We are also here to help others walk their own positive paths of spiritual growth. We may not always see the purpose in what we are doing—nonetheless, it's our mission to try to figure it out. In life, we are happiest when our goals are in alignment with our purpose and life assignments.

Whenever I talk to my wise mother about something I am planning to do, she almost inevitably reminds me to make sure that there is a purpose to what I am doing. Here is my mother's prayer: God, if there is no purpose in what is happening right now, help me walk away from it. I surrender to your will and to your purpose in my life. I am ready for what is next.

Padre, si no tiene propósito por favor aléjame de esto.

Padre, me rindo a Ti y a Tu propósito en mi vida. Estoy lista para lo que sigue.

Pause for Just a Moment to Think About Your Purpose

A significant part of the mystery of life involves our finding ourselves, knowing that in each of our lives there will be different seasons and challenges as well as different opportunities for fulfillment and happiness. We are all going to be presented with gazillions of choices and possibilities. Train yourself to keep your purpose at the forefront of your mind. Before making any decisions or doing anything, pause for a moment to remember your values and honor your purpose. If something you are doing or planning to do isn't fulfilling your values or purpose, remind yourself to stop and walk away. Life will always present new opportunities. My experiences have shown me that I want to invite more love and less drama into my life. I want to be able to walk away from negativity and complaining and focus more on the positive—learning, doing, and loving.

Never forget that our time here on Earth is limited. We are here to live and learn, but we are also here to serve. We all have wisdom to share, and your voice can have an impact in helping others. The simplest acts of kindness and compassion will improve another person's experience.

Be Prepared for the Ups and Downs of Life

None of us are exempt from rough times and tough challenges. Sh*t happens, and it can wear on us, making us feel down and defeated. Whenever you feel challenged by events in your life, it helps to remember that you are going through a growth cycle and there is a lesson for you to figure out. It's how you react to your ups and downs that will determine your future.

One of the first lessons I needed to learn: Don't give up.

In my own life, whenever I feel most depleted and stuck, I have found it helpful to reach out to do something that challenges me and gets me moving. I remember one time when I felt really stuck. My energy was extremely low, and I felt defeated and uninspired. I needed to create some kind of shift in my attitude and I didn't want to fall back on old behaviors, like my own personal favorite of hiding out in my bed. With that in mind, I signed up for an afternoon workshop with a coach who had some unusual techniques for helping people break through the barriers in their minds.

Everyone in the workshop was given a board that was maybe a foot square and more than a half inch thick. Following the coach's instructions, on one side of the board I wrote down all the things I wanted to accomplish in life. When I looked around the room, I could see that, like me, all the other participants were writing down their goals of achieving better relationships, work situations, more money, and successful outcomes. On the other side of the board, we wrote down all our frustrations and fears about achieving our goals. These were the things standing in the way of where we wanted to be.

The coach told us that we were first going to meditate, and we were then going to use our hands to break through the side of the board with all our frustrations and fears to reach the side that represented our goals.

I remember looking at that board and thinking, How the hell am I going to punch through that? I didn't know if I was strong enough to break through a board with my hands. Almost in response to my thoughts, the coach reminded us that we had to stop thinking negatively. We had to keep telling ourselves that we would be able to accomplish our goal, and, in the process, we needed to let go of all the stories we were creating about how we were not going to be able to do it.

There have been so many times when I'm tempted to give up without really trying. The effort seems too great, and I'm concerned that I'm not strong enough. For a moment there in that workshop, as I stared at the board with my goals written on one side and my challenges on the other, I got caught up in negative and self-defeating thoughts, and that's exactly how I felt. But I also knew that I didn't really want to give up.

Following the coach's instructions, I positioned my hand, and then, on the count of three, using all my physical and mental energy, I hit the board. And it snapped! I felt an amazing sense of empowerment. Those times when I feel most defeated, I remember that moment when the board snapped. I tell myself, "You can do it!" and I keep moving forward.

Facing My Biggest Personal Challenge

When my goal of becoming a model was first taking shape, I had no idea how to go about achieving it. I had enormous physical challenges, like my actual weight, but my psychological and emotional challenges were just as great. Up until that point, my life had been filled with too many poorly thought-out choices and missteps. I was lugging around more than my physical weight in emotional garbage—old resentments, shame, anger, and guilt about the past as well as uncertainty, fear, and anxiety about the future.

I also had a ton of questions about my life: Why did I have so many failed romantic relationships? Why were the wrong men drawn to me? Why had infidelity been an issue in all my relationships? Why was I such an emotional eater? Why did I have so much anxiety about so many things? When I was nervous about something, why was I so quick to go into panic mode, complete with shaking hands and hyperventilation? Why was I so worried about people making fun of me, and what could I do to change my reactions? Why did I have such an intense fear of failure—fear that I wouldn't be able to succeed at a career as well as fear that I would never find a relationship like the one my parents shared? I was incredibly stressed financially and always worried about money and my ability to pay for all the things my kids needed. And then, once again, there was the reality of the size of my body! The odds were good that, unless I did something, I would develop a weight-related illness or disability. I was terrified that I was going to end up being a burden to my children. The challenges that life throws at us are designed to help us figure out and find purpose in life—who we are and what we are meant to be doing. I knew that I couldn't rewrite my past, but what could I do to improve my present and create a different outlook for my future?

My life started to change at twenty-eight, when I was diagnosed with a brain cyst. I had become so sick that I felt as though I wasn't going to make it. I had to get serious about fixing my life. For starters, I needed to make a conscious effort to get rid of my toxic thinking. I had to shed all the old resentments and anger that I was dragging around with me. They were weighing down my spirit and creating havoc with my life. I'm not the first person who has said that anger can manifest itself in our bodies or that holding on to rage and resentment can damage our health.

Hard realization: Wallowing in the remembered pain of my negative experiences was making me ill—very ill!

I had spent way too much time thinking about, not to mention crying over, bad things that had happened. I was the mother of three young children. My life was at stake, and I had to find a different way to handle unhappiness. I decided that I would make a conscious effort to condition my mind. Every time I had a painful, angry, or resentful thought, I would talk myself through it. For example, every time I remembered a particularly unhappy moment in my history, my usual tendency was to cry and keep going over the details of what had happened, remembering how hurt and upset I had felt. Doing this made me even more hurt and upset. I was determined to end this pattern of thinking!

My decision: I wasn't going to allow toxic memories from my past to continue to hurt and poison me again and again.

Every time a painful memory crossed my mind, I told myself to let it go. I allowed myself to feel the emotion in that moment, and then I made a conscious decision to let it go with love. Instead of ruminating about the unhappy memory, I forced myself to think of something pleasant and good. In my life, for example, I gave birth to each of my three children without a loving partner by my side. Thinking about how sad and alone I felt during those times in the hospital would almost inevitably make me feel sorry for myself, and I would start sobbing and then spend the rest of the day nursing my pain. Well, I forced myself to change the memory. Instead of focusing on my emotional pain at those moments, I would think about each of my children—their first smiles and how much I loved them. I would remember the good moments of parenting, and this would release my pain. Instead of crying, I would smile.

My choice: I was going to redirect my emotions.

There were so many times in the day when I felt frustrated and unhappy. I realized that I had to train myself to look at those moments in a more positive light. Let's say I was frustrated because my son Valentino's therapy wasn't going as well as I wanted; instead of focusing on the frustration, I could tell myself to remember how far he had come and how much he had improved. Instead of feeling frustration, I could feel pride and joy in his accomplishments. Let's say I was having a physically bad day and was feeling less than steady on my feet. Instead of becoming angry, anxious, and annoyed, I could focus on how much my health had improved and how fortunate I was to have wonderful parents to support me. Instead of feeling sorry for myself because I didn't have a romantic partner, I could feel joy in knowing that I was free and independent, nobody was telling me what to do or not do, and the world was full of good, boundless opportunities for my future.

I knew in my gut that my anger and resentment were factors in my being sick. Hanging on to these emotions was not worth the price of health or sacrificing my purpose. I made a decision: These negative emotions had to go, and I had to change.

Finding a New Approach: No More Playing the Victim

When I was younger, it was very easy for me to view myself as a victim. I hate to admit it, but when I think about it, "I'm the victim" had definitely become my fallback position.

The kids at school were mean to me—"I'm the victim."

My metabolism and genetics make it easy for me to gain weight—"I'm the victim."

The men in my life have all abandoned me—"I'm the victim."

My children are growing up without fathers—"I'm the victim."

My son has cerebral palsy—"I'm the victim."

I've never had a good, trustworthy romantic relationship—"I'm the victim."

Owning My Life!

I am not a victim!

I absolutely believe that I have to be completely honest with myself—and others—about the role I've personally played in everything that has happened in my life. No question about it: My issues included some monumentally sh*tty decisions. These decisions had frequently been made because of my quest for love and validation. I always wanted a marriage like my parents had and foolishly believed that if I wasn't in a committed relationship by a certain age, not only was I a failure, it was never going to happen.

It's all too easy to sit around feeling victimized and sorry for yourself. And I definitely had a great deal of practice in doing just that. I was learning that all the times I felt self-pity, I was fanning and feeding all my feelings of low self-esteem. I had to change. I had to redirect my mind and stop myself from going over and over all the bad memories. I had to stop crying about my struggles and my losses. I learned to allow myself to feel the feeling and then let it go. My life was at stake—I had to lose my "poor me" mentality. It was time for action and not tears.

My first step was acknowledging what I had been doing. The second was to make a commitment to do things differently. When I woke up every morning, I determined that I would no longer focus on the pain I had felt in my past. Instead, I would corral all the good memories and moments in my life. I would think about them and remind myself to feel gratitude.

Saved by the Library, the Internet, and the Self-Help Section at Barnes & Noble

As I struggled to change my attitude, I had a great deal of help from some truly inspirational writers and thinkers. When I was trying to get more information about my physical problems, I stumbled (literally) into the self-help section at Barnes & Noble where my formal search for answers began. And I began reading. I learned a great deal: I was obviously not the first person who was facing life challenges. I was not the first person to feel depressed and alone. I was not the first woman with a history of unhappy romantic choices, and I was not the first woman who wanted to create change in her life. People who understood what I was experiencing had written books and articles and given interviews that could help me change my life.

Which men and women helped change my life? Let's start with Deepak Chopra, Iyanla Vanzant, Wayne Dyer, and, of course, Oprah Winfrey. These are some of the people who I believed were able to understand my pain and helped me find a path to a healthier, more positive point of view. Everything I read and heard from these inspirational thinkers started making tremendous sense. My reading wasn't casual. It was purposeful as well as informing and life-changing. I took it seriously. If I read a sentence that applied to me, I wrote it down, studied it, and worked at putting it into practice. I made a list of ways in which I had to change my attitude. At the top of my list I wrote:

Learn to become grateful.

Learn to become forgiving.

Was it easy? No. Even when working as a life coach, I sometimes find myself talking to a client about a truth that I knew in my soul was important for them to "get," hearing a bell ringing: "Ding! Ding! Ding! Yo, Rosie! You are talking to *yourself*!!!" It's a lifelong process of reflecting and recalibrating and always trying to steer a straighter course. I know that even though I'm now trying to help others in my position, I realize I still have work to do on *me*.

Learning to Become More Grateful

Feeling grateful is the direct opposite of feeling victimized. If I was going to get healthy and change my life, it was important for me to recognize all the ways in which I had been very blessed and all the things about which I needed to feel grateful. It was time for me to acknowledge and embrace the beauty of the universe.

For a time, when I was still in my twenties, I was totally convinced that I was going to die. As I got better, I couldn't help but feel grateful that I was still breathing and that slowly but surely I was beginning to be able to talk without slurring my words and walking without hanging on to someone or something. I was grateful, and I purposefully decided that I wasn't going to let that feeling go. I wasn't going to allow negativity to find its way back into my thoughts. Feeling grateful helps us expand our lives; it helps us open up and allow good people and experiences into our lives. I had learned the hard way that if you hold negative feelings about yourself—as in "I am a victim"—this negativity is exactly what you will invite into your life.

Slowly, but surely, I was beginning to get rid of all the destructive energy that had been beating me up.

Learning to Become More Forgiving

Oh yes, forgiveness. It wouldn't be so difficult to forgive the random people who had hurt me—the people who had briefly passed through my life without really touching my heart. But could I forgive the men I had loved? Could I forgive my daughter's father for turning my life upside down and then abandoning me? How about my ex-husbands? Could I forgive and forget all the ways I felt I had been mistreated by life? Could I forgive myself? I realized that I had allowed all those things to happen. And I knew intuitively that my failure to forgive the past was keeping me stuck in the pain and resentment I was feeling in the moment. My mental and physical well-being were at stake.

In my fantasy life, when I was feeling sorriest for myself, I would sometimes imagine a scenario where one of the people who hurt me would stumble through the door and beg my forgiveness. We've all had thoughts like these. And let's face it, my ego loved that scenario and the idea of seeing them on their knees, sobbing with regret for what they had done to me. An example of ego, ego, ego hard at work. Even if there was a chance that it would ever happen, I knew it wouldn't have changed the past or made a difference in the future. So I had to tell my ego to back off and focus on my genuine healing. **It was time for me to work on my ability to practice unconditional forgiveness.**

At first, of course, I resisted doing this. There are reasons why all of us get stuck in our feelings of pain and unhappiness. And *damn*, it's hard to just free those who have hurt us, releasing any thought of obligation we are mentally holding about what they *owe* us—what we need to get from them emotionally before we call it even. But I had to let old resentments and pain go and focus on the bigger picture. I had to do it all for me and my sanity—not for anybody else.

I was alive and breathing! *Hallelujah!*

I had options, possibilities, and purpose! Wow!

And I had dreams! So many dreams!

I couldn't let my emotional pain keep me from making the most of my life. And learning to forgive was one of the most important steps on my journey—and one of the hardest. It was important for other reasons as well. My children, like all children, would have a tendency to mirror how I reacted to situations. I wanted them to move forward without the baggage of my pain. My ability to forgive and let go would set a better and healthier standard for the quality of their relationships. I can already see this in my daughter, Bella. When she was younger, she would sometimes ask about her father. Why did he leave? Why did he abandon us? Why did he not love me? Her questions were similar to mine, which is a big red flag. Now she is able to say, "Everything happens for a reason. God bless my father, wherever he may be."

Some thoughts about the people who hurt us: Let go of your memories about the pain they caused you. Think about it this way: There is good in every person who hurt you, no matter what they did or how they did it. They may not have been expressing the best versions of themselves. Keep in mind that hurtful people are often acting out of their own pain and insecurity. Recognize that we are not always showing the best versions of ourselves. Acknowledge that you were hurt, and in your head, thank the people who hurt you for the lessons, and let that hurt go.

Unconditional Forgiveness Becomes Transformational Forgiveness

This is important! There are different types of forgiveness. We all understand what it means to forgive the person who apologizes to us. But there are many times in life when we will never receive any apologies. Many, if not all, of us have been in situations where we have been vulnerable, giving our hearts and our trust, and then ending up being emotionally body-punched and totally slammed to the ground. We don't fully understand what happened; we don't know what we did wrong; and we will probably never get any answers.

I've learned that it's essential to be able to forgive and move on—even when there are no apologies or answers. You have to accept that nothing will ever be resolved. However, your sanity is at stake, so you have to let go of the hurt and move on. You have to stop thinking about hurtful people or situations. Being able to forgive even when there are no apologies and your heart is still filled with unanswered questions can be transformative. Yes, you can create a new and better life! You are giving this kind of forgiveness for your own good because you are able to be more focused on creating peace in your own life. Plato was an ancient Greek philosopher who lived in the fifth century BC. Here's a quote that's often attributed to him:

Be kind, for everyone you meet is fighting a hard battle.

An affirmation: I am not what happened to me. I am what I choose to become. I choose to forgive and let you go with love. And today I choose to love myself for everything that I am.

Take a deep breath. Breathe out, and let it go! It's time to close the doors to the past.

Stand up and create a new truth for yourself! Are you ready to lead your best life? The best is yet to come.

A Final Thought

It's your responsibility to fulfill your dream. Nothing can stop your destiny.

> *I can do all this through Him who gives me strength.*
>
> PHILIPPIANS 4:13 (NIV)

Dedication

TO MY EXTRAORDINARY PARENTS! HOW MANY WAYS CAN I thank you for loving me unconditionally? You personified integrity and consistently demonstrated the important values that I now live by. You have always been supportive of everything I do, and, yes, I'm so sorry for all the headaches and worries I made you go through. Dad, you taught me the importance of persistence and proved to me on a daily basis that strong, loving, faithful men do exist. Mom, you always showed me and the world grace, love, kindness, and wisdom. Thank you for never abandoning me, even in my moments of genuine stupidity. My ongoing prayer to God is one of thanks for both of you and the love you have showed me throughout my life. May God always give you favor, grace, and a long, healthy life.

To my kids—Bella, Valentino, and Alex: You reminded me not to give up and loved me even when I didn't love myself. Always remember how much I love you, although there were times I didn't show it in a way you could understand. Nothing really prepares you for how to be an excellent parent or provides a how-to manual on how to do everything right. I realize I made tons of mistakes, and I'm sorry. I was a young, inexperienced parent. Throughout my pain and growth, I was learning how to love myself as well as learning how to show you how much I loved all of you. I pray God gives you wisdom and protection throughout your life and that your experiences take you to a place where you are able to serve others as a way of healing and sharing your love. I love you! I love you! I love you!

To Gilbert, my husband: You showed me that it is safe to love again. You loved me despite my emotional wounds and held my hand through my process of healing, always teaching that it is more than okay to be vulnerable, helping me gain the courage to love another human being, regardless of past experience. You helped me know that I am lovable! You are my answered prayer, and I am blessed that God sent you my way. And now a special and wonderful thank-you for sharing the gift of our new son, Emiliano.

To Alexandra Boos, my prayer partner, friend, and manager: Mama, you have been with me during my ups and downs since Day One, and you have kindly called me out on my sh*t when I needed it, but always from a place of love. We have celebrated, cried, and prayed our way through and now we manifest this after so many years! THANK YOU FOR WALKING THIS JOURNEY WITH ME UNCONDITIONALLY AND ALWAYS speaking LIFE over me when no one believed in me!

I also want to remember my precious nephew, Orlando, who died too young and always smiled no matter how deep his pain. I want to thank you, Lolo, for teaching me to be more compassionate and reminding me that our time on this earth is not eternal. You're an angel who brought many lessons to my life. I get chills every time I am reminded of you! I think about you whenever I see a hummingbird in the garden and every time I see your little sister's eyes. I love you, Lolo. *Que Dios te tenga en su Gloria!*

And to the indelible memory of Carlos: You introduced me to my love of dance and taught me the importance of having a heart full of love—despite people's unkind words and actions! You showed me how to let go and dance, even when I cried. Carlos, you always taught me that my inner beauty was what counted the most while also helping me gain confidence in my own skin. You listened to me and always made me feel beautiful. You transformed my soul and my vision for what beauty truly means! I miss you so much!

Acknowledgments

THANK YOU FIRST TO GOD, FOR ALL THE OPPORTUNITIES AND lessons learned.

I want to start by thanking my brother Joe, his wife Nancy, and my sisters Lily and Priscilla. Although you didn't always understand my dreams, you always provided loving support as well as lots of laughter. I will always love you. I want to honor my late grandmothers, Maria and Mercedes, two strong and incredible women, for teaching me that we are all human and that each of us has a special and unique story to tell. As a child, I didn't realize all you went through, but I can see it now. I also want to honor and remember my late grandfather, Patricio Mercado: you were an angel who always "showed up" to save my family whenever we needed you. And I can't forget Sofia and Nick: thank you for allowing me to be a part of your lives and for opening your hearts to create a new family

There have been so many people and blessings for which I will always be grateful. My dreams would not have come true without

Gwen Devoe, the strong woman who gave me my first modeling break; you accepted me for who I was regardless of my size and allowed me to walk that first runway. I can never forget the amazing Oscar Picazo, who I've come to think of as family. You took the photographs that changed my life and continue to be an incredible support in my career. I also owe a great deal to the following people with extraordinary talents: Makeup and Hair by Zee; Steven Tambia; Jennifer Arias; makeup artist, Andrea Vanessa Cardenas; wardrobe stylists, Larissa Tailor and Tom Soluri; skin care expert Leslie Estevez; New Life Med Solutions; powerful Latino publicist Lee Hernandez; and Justin Blum of Raw Fitness, who taught me to discover my own physical strength; you pushed me even when I didn't want to keep going.

I will always remember the people who inspired my career and opened doors, allowing me to step through: correspondent Luis Sandoval; producer Luz Maria Doria; and journalist Maria Antonietta Collins; your courageous story of weight loss directly impacted mine.

Health is the most important thing we have and I want to thank the wonderful doctors who were instrumental in my being able to transform my body and my health: Dr. Bernie Hanna; Dr. Ivan Cuevas; Iyanla Vanzant; and Dr. Carlos Buenrostro, whose kindness and compassion was key to my transformation.

I am forever grateful to all the mentors, teachers, and inspirational women and men who helped me walk my path. You changed me by sharing your wisdom, encouraging me through the dark places in my life: Jay Shetty; Lewis Howes; Tony Robbins; Gary

Vee; Dr. Wayne Dyer; and Panache Desai, for guiding me through my deepest anxieties and teaching me that I am not broken. Thank you also to Jerry Metellus for teaching me how to use my voice in a powerful and respectful way.

Thank you to my publishing support system: Stephany Evans, my agent: I completely appreciate your strength in fighting to get my story told; Julia Sokol Coopersmith for "hanging in" with me. The process was not always easy, but I'm grateful to God for putting you in my life to help me get through it; I also want to thank everyone at HarperOne, especially Gideon Weil and Sydney Rogers, who gave me the opportunity to tell my story—with a special thanks to Sydney, an amazing editor who helped me do it in a real and authentic way. I also want to thank everyone at HarperOne and HarperCollins Español especially Judith Curr, Edward Benitez, and Emily Strode. And Jairo Pardo for his careful guidance.

Behind every dream, there is a team, and I'm grateful for my entertainment lawyer, Richard Corey, Marki Costello for being an incredible hosting teacher, and Mark Turner for always looking for good opportunities. And I can't forget John Undeland, who always provides solid counsel, wisdom, and advice.

I will always be grateful to Dr. Phil for allowing me to be a special correspondent on his show. Honestly, it was a dream come true. And I will always remember Robin McGraw for all her kindness. I also need to acknowledge and thank Judy Sanchez for giving me the opportunity to voice my opinion and thoughts as well as Carla Pennington, Patricia Ciano, and Jay McGraw for giving me my first big hosting break and helping me grow in that process. Also thanks to Rob Shieffele and other members of Stage 29 Productions. I owe so much to Chava Gomez and Angel Maciel, my first media teachers.

I'll never forget the empowering women at Face the Truth: Vivica Fox, Dr. Judy Ho, Areva Martin, Judge "Scary Mary" Chrzanowski. Each of you taught me something about myself and the business, for which I will always be grateful. Thank you for your patience and understanding as I was growing on the job.

And I don't have enough ways to say thank-you to Fatima and Miss Linda Lewis for always showing Valentino so much patience and love. Fatima, I will always be grateful that you were there to be my second set of eyes.

About the Author

ROSIE MERCADO is a nationally recognized television personality and thought leader. At twenty-eight, Rosie was 420 pounds, underemployed, multi-divorced, and a mother of three children. And then, something amazing happened. Rosie turned her life around, losing more than two hundred pounds and becoming a professional model, television co-host, life coach, and motivational speaker. Articles about Rosie have appeared in a variety of outlets, including *People, Forbes, TMZ, Daily Mail, Cosmopolitan,* and *Bustle.* A proud bilingual Latina who was recently named as one of *People en Español*'s twenty-five most powerful Latinas, Rosie is a true crossover star who also guest-hosts and is a correspondent on the leading Spanish-language networks Telemundo and Univision, as well as on *Dr. Phil* and *The Doctors.*

Rosie, who splits her time between Las Vegas and Southern California, spends every day advocating for people who are marginalized, transforming societal norms so that all are valued and accepted. Her remarkable story of achievement should be read by all those who crave change and are struggling to lead more purpose-driven lives.